Creating Money

spiritual prescriptions for prosperity

Also by the author

The Seven Rays
Psychic Self-Defense

Creating Money

spiritual prescriptions for prosperity

Samantha Stevens

INSOMNIAC PRESS

Library and Archives Canada Cataloguing in Publication

Stevens, Samantha, 1960-
        Creating money : spiritual presecriptions for prosperity / Samantha Stevens.

ISBN 1-894663-71-3

        1. Wealth—Religious aspects. I. Title.

BL65.W42S72 2004   304'.4   C2004-903948-2

The publisher gratefully acknowledges the support of the Canada Council, the Ontario Arts Council and the Department of Canadian Heritage through the Book Publishing Industry Development Program.

Printed and bound in Canada

Insomniac Press
192 Spadina Avenue, Suite 403
Toronto, Ontario, Canada, M5T 2C2
www.insomniacpress.com

Table of Contents

Introduction

What is Prosperity?

Prosperity is not so much about having tons of money in the bank; it is about having a balanced life. The four cornerstones of the foundation of Prosperity are health, freedom, happiness and love. Without each of these cornerstones in place, chaos will rule in your personal life and finances.

Although this book is about trying to create or manifest money, it is important to realize that actual prosperity is different than perceived prosperity. Actual prosperity is the result of actions based on truths that satiate the soul. When you have peace of mind, you are basking in a state of actual prosperity. Perceived prosperity is when you have the home, the car and all the trappings of success, yet still feel sick or empty inside. You can become rich by robbing others, but all you will be is a successful thief.

Most of us perceive prosperity as something that requires sacrifice. A common belief is that in order to get rich we must practice the fine art of compensation. This misconception is at work in many people's lives as we short-circuit our health, self-respect and time in order to create all the money we think we need to solve our problems. We live under the mass belief that money cannot be earned without some measure of self-sabotage. But if prosperity has cost us in any way, then we are not truly prosperous.

True prosperity is not about possessions. It is about generating a cycle of energy that easily regenerates to create more money. Though money is a tool or an energy that can be used to create prosperity, part of its purpose is to be let go in order to be recalculated in the world. To be truly prosperous, the temple of your soul must also welcome the well-being and happiness of others, or your coffers will be truly empty. People are often the source of your prosperity. People are not attracted to a sick, unhappy or lonely person. They are attracted to a person who has the faith and conviction that for every demand there is a supply from the universe. People who are money magnets also tend to take care of their health, can see options where others see none, find happiness in living in the present and give love freely without expecting approval in return.

If you are anxious about or attached to money, then you will only attract more anxiety into your life. If you see money as evil or something that must be slaved for, then you are likely to be oppressed by debt or work endlessly for profit.

If you believe in the notion that "the rich get richer and the poor get poorer," you are writing a disaster script that you will probably follow your entire life.

Prosperity is about perceiving and believing that you live in a benevolent universe where there is a supply for every demand. It is about faith in your own ability to create a successful life script for yourself by seeing the world you live in as a place that is filled with unlimited opportunity. Before you can put your finances in order, you need to order your perceptions, so that everything is put in perfect perspective, like the Rule of the Golden Mean in painting.

The great yogis would say that if you are worried about money, then you are not truly rich. To be truly prosperous you have to develop a lack of attachment to money and possessions. The only things of value that you have are those qualities that you take with you when you die.

Chapter One

Manna From Heaven and Other Miracles

"Miracles come from above," but mostly, miracles come from within. The manifestation of a miraculous event comes from your ability to train the imaging faculty of the mind. As the Greeks said, "Know thyself."

The mind is divided into three sections: the conscious, the subconscious and the super-conscious.

The conscious mind, also known as the carnal or mortal mind, is responsible for most of our perceptions of life. It is the part of the mind that has thoughts, either positive or negative, and is subtly programmed by our health, emotions and desires.

The subconscious mind can be compared to a great storehouse of primal and archetypical images. This is the source of imagination and dreams. The subconscious mind is easily impressed by thoughts from the conscious mind—creating both fears and hopes.

The super-conscious mind is the "God Mind" that Plato often spoke of and that connects us all to each other and the Divine Source of Spirit. It is the place where your Higher Self, which is like a hologram of God or a Higher Power, urges you to attain perfection and true love. It is the home of the imagination.

It is the conscious mind that impresses the subconscious with its visions of disease, poverty and disaster. The trick is to train your imagination, which is connected to your God Mind, to envision a world full of possibilities.

Money Is an Energy

Nothing can be created from a subconcious mind that is poisoned by impressions of poverty, anxiety, fear, self-doubt, resentment, jealousy or self-pity. In fact, fear of poverty can bring on the actual condition as this fear demonstrates a lack of faith in the super-conscious self to bring about a supply for every demand.

Have you ever noticed how easy it is to have a small wish fulfilled rather than a large wish? Usually this kind of small wish is for something like a pair of shoes. Remarkably, most of us just have to think of the desired item briefly and within a few days it seems to pop into our lives. This is an example of how the super-conscious self creates a supply for every demand.

The reason that larger wishes, such as "I wish I could pay off my mortgage," are not fulfilled is because the impression of the desire that we send to our subconscious is usually attached to a great deal of anxiety. This is like attaching weights to our wishes so that they sink to the bottom of the pond of our subconscious. Another illustration that the universe supplies us with our demands is the scenario in which we lose something and then, much to our surprise, the lost object is replaced a few days later. It may not be the exact same item, but it is usually similar and arrives in the form of a gift. Usually this is the kind of loss, such as that of a broken vase, that we accept easily with a shrug of the shoulders.

Unfortunately most people equate money with a sense of loss because we are always paying bills or letting go of the money with resentment. We are taught from an early age to think that money is something to be hoarded until it is wrestled from our cold dead hands. We are told things like "money doesn't grow on trees" when in reality, it does! It's made from paper.

Since money is an energy symbolized by the financial events that take place around us, it is important to think about it responsibly. We cannot necessarily control

our subconscious mind, but we can train our consciou
mind by appealing to the super-conscious (our perfec
self that is made in the image of God) to help.

This means we must always use our imaging facultie
to picture for ourselves the best case financial scenari
Some people are so battered by debt, deadlines an
responsibilities that they have lost sight of their life's pur
pose. Through meditation, prayer, positive affirmation
and creative visualizations, you can spark the imagina
tion into creating a picture of the path you must take
Creating this positive picture is called inspiration.

However, you must do more than just picture th
path; you must also follow through on your intuitions i
a practical way. If you are inspired to make a list c
things to do, for example, it is not enough just to mak
the list and then shrug your shoulders and say, "The uni
verse will take care of it."

You must also question each intuition to ensure tha
it has not been colored by irrational thoughts from th
subconscious mind. Remember that your prosperit
temple is built on order, not chaos, and based on plan
that fit in with your grand design.

The subconscious can be a bit of a booby trap. It is th
part of the mind that presents a "no" to your ever
"yes". Whenever you suggest a thought to the subcon
scious mind, it acts as a Devil's Advocate and present
counter images of why your dreams are not possible
Usually, the subconscious mind has been initially
impressed by rational thoughts from your consciou
self, which is concerned with self-preservation and sur
vival. The subconscious mind's primary purpose is to
destroy anything that it perceives to be out of balance ir
the cosmos. This is why too much focus on money mat
ters can often cause financial disaster.

Money itself operates on a low vibration in the astral spheres. Prosperity, which includes such states as happiness, freedom, health and love, operates on a higher sphere.

Cash is not something meant to be possessed forever. It is an energy that circulates through the universe, aggregating and multiplying in the positive and the negative. If money is not flowing in and out of your life it means that the well of your subconscious is poisoned or dried up. You are literally out of the gas you need to fuel the imagination. The subconscious is like a beast that must be tamed to make it work for your imagination, not against it. You need to produce angels, not monsters, in your astral financial sphere.

The first simple step you can take is to change your thoughts about money. There is an old saying that goes, "Change the thought, change the feeling." You need to impress positive thoughts upon your subconscious mind. The cosmos is a benevolent place that encourages growth, and if there is a death, that death is usually replaced by its equivalent or better. When it comes to money, it is important to remember that it is finite. Your capacity to attract or make money is as infinite as your Divine Imagination.

It is difficult to impress thoughts of prosperity upon a subconscious mind that is already in turmoil. A disturbed subconscious creates distorted perceptions about money. This is why it is important to take care of those states of being that form the four cornerstones of prosperity: health, freedom, happiness and love. Notice that these cornerstones are not possessions. If you are not healthy, act healthy. If you are not free, act as if you have choices. If you are not happy, put on a smile. If you are not loved, give more love to others. When it comes to prosperity two cliches do apply: "Fake it till you make it," and "supply to others what you lack in yourself." That is why when a client complains of poverty I immediately suggest that he or she "get out of self" by performing a charitable act for others. The client's fearful conscious self is casting a shadow over his or her path. Even though it is just a shadow, it has fooled the person into thinking it is an insurmountable obstacle.

The idea is to raise your spiritual vibration by transcending negative thoughts so that you attract the situations you need at the right time. This usually involves focusing your attention on positive goals and aligning your heart with your will. Various cultures suggest different ways to raise your vibration (as will be discussed later in greater detail).

The Word Is Flesh

If you ask for success and prepare for failure, you will fail. You are only capable of receiving what you are capable of envisioning for yourself.

The great visionary Florence Scovel Shinn called the imagination the "scissors of the mind." She described how the imagination takes what the individual pictures and cuts it up so that it fits in with his or her perception of reality. However, people's perceptions about money might not necessarily reflect the reality of their financial situation. For instance, the woman living on credit cards feels rich, but she is actually poor.

One way to train the imagination so that you picture only the best for yourself is to watch your conversation carefully. The subconscious mind is like a vacuum cleaner that sucks up all the labels we have for money and stores them for future self-sabotage.

For instance, if you find yourself saying "I am always

broke," you will find yourself manifesting this situation over and over as the subconscious mind associates that phrase with the word "money." Some writers of positive affirmations believe that the subconscious mind does not pick up negative words like in the phrase "I'm not poor." The subconscious hears the "I'm" and the "poor" but ignores the "not." That is why it is important, if you are writing positive affirmations, to phrase them in the present and in the positive, for example: "I am rich."

Every time you make a negative remark about money, such as "It is impossible to get ahead," or "The wolves are at the door," you are adding negativity not only to your subconscious but to the collective unconsciousness that unites us all. You are, in effect, poisoning the very wells from which the fountains of prosperity spring.

If you like, picture the subconscious mind like a bank that is linked to a mass economy. Each word you deposit into your mind, especially when you speak the word out loud, is like making a credit to your spiritual bank account.

Unfortunately, for most people the subject of money is usually associated with negative situations. This is why it is important not to pay attention to headlines or statistics in the newspapers. For instance, if you read a statistic such as "50% of women over forty experience a drop in income," you might want to automatically correct the statement by saying "I transcend statistics. I have potential."

Also, be careful how you describe your financial position to others. You don't want people's negative perceptions about you to compound the interest on your spiritual debt.

Words state your beliefs, and beliefs express a conviction that something is happening or is going to happen. Talking about worst case scenarios is bad financial practice as it demonstrates a lack of faith that the universe provides a supply for every demand.

It is important to examine what you demand from the universe every day. Examine what you have to offer the universe as well. If you look at the circulation of energy as an economy, what do you have to offer the universe in exchange for its graces? Do you behave like a needy child that demands to be taken care of, or do you constructively "report to the carpet" every day for duty? Are you a star in life, or a black hole that sucks up negative energy from others?

If your finances are careening out of control and poverty and limitation influence all aspects of your life, it is time for you to become very still. Your subconscious mind has become a rolling snowball, gathering more and more negativity, creating an avalanche of negative financial events in your life. The only way to control such a situation is to clear your mind of all negative thoughts and anxieties and to meditate until you feel a sense of calm.

Miracles tend to happen at that juncture between rest and motion. You must stay still so that your Higher Self can catch and save you. When we are panicky, most of us run from our Higher Selves as we become convinced that the Divine Order does not have our highest good in mind. Sometimes this "rescue" happens randomly, like a flash of inspiration telling you exactly what to do to get yourself out of the situation.

If after meditating you still don't have an answer, practice the "First Things First" rule. Clear your mind of all anxieties and try to think about what you can do in the next five minutes, even if it is as simple as doing dishes so that the kitchen looks nicer. Even this small step can help clear the clutter and chaos so antithetical to the clarity that attracts prosperity. Any activity that gets your mind off the negative subject gets the unproductive thoughts out of the way so the Universe can work on solving your problem. In the words of Paul McCartney, "There will be an answer...let it be."

The Law of Circulation

The quality of money is fluid, rather than static, which is why money is so often compared to water. We use such phrases as "trickle of income," "a wave of prosperity" or "being drained of funds."

For many, managing money can be compared to weathering stormy seas. Very few of us watch our ship come in over calm water. We usually have to manipulate and navigate our way through a storm. This is particularly true of people who live paycheck to paycheck. Other individuals are capable of manifesting a lot of cash, only to watch it go out as fast as it came in, like a river that periodically floods and dries up. Other people find themselves facing a dam, constantly waiting for checks that never seem to arrive on time. Each of these watery scenarios is a metaphor for a spiritual malaise that can cause a lack of money in your life.

People who experience a trickle of income probably have little faith that the Universe possesses an abundant supply. They also usually demand more from others than they put out in terms of astral energy. People who expect to be taken care of without acting for themselves often find their cash flow reduced.

Individuals who borrow from Peter to pay Paul fit the whirlpool metaphor. This type of individual usually has a deep-seated belief that his or her ability to create cash is limited and that "you are damned if you do and damned if you don't." A fear of success or prosperity might also be behind the construction of such a financial picture.

If you are being drained of funds, then you probably hold the subconscious belief that you somehow don't deserve to have money, or that you must pay and pay just to exist! Low self-esteem and a lack of confidence usually cause this condition.

Those who experience great ups and downs in their finances are also putting out a vibration that says, "I don't deserve my money. Prosperity must cost me." These people feel as if fate, rather then their Higher Selves, is somehow responsible for their finances.

Individuals who feel they are facing a dam that is blocking the source are putting out a vibration that says, "Money is a problem." This kind of individual was usually raised to believe that money is the root of all evil, or that "good things happen to those who wait." These people need the flexibility of faith to believe that "good things happen to people who don't have to wait" as well.

There are subtle ways you can ease these negative thoughts, particularly if you don't have any money at all. The first way is to practice an attitude of gratitude. Each time a bill arrives, thank the Universe for the faith that you can and you will pay that bill. You would be in a supremely bad position if you did not receive any bills at all, since that would mean you are not considered part of the energy that circulates around prosperity.

All the great world religions recommend the practice of tithing, or giving 10% of everything you earn to charity, freely and anonymously. This replenishes the well of prosperity.

I find the metaphor of water to be useful when it comes to managing money. If someone or something is draining your finances, plug the drain. If you don't have enough money, find a way to turn on the tap so you can fill your tub of plenty. If your money situation is stagnant, then stir up the waters a bit, either by giving money freely or by blessing your bills as they go out of the house.

It Is Always Darkest Before the Dawn

"Fear" is a word you don't ever want your subconscious mind to associate with money. Yet many of us experience fear when we don't have enough to make ends meet.

When you are afraid you are not united with your Higher Self. You are of two minds. Fear demonstrates a belief in two potentialities, one good and one evil. If you eliminate fear of the future from your life, then your subconscious can only manifest events from one inevitability: the good.

You must be careful of what others say to you. People can invite loss, fear, disaster and sickness into your life simply by expressing their anxiety about such matters. If someone calls you up to participate in a "woe-is-me" festival, simply say "no thank you." Such a practice is essential to your financial health, especially if you are dealing with a crisis. When you experience a crisis it can be difficult to have faith that your prayers will be answered. But the fact that such an overwhelming situation exists is actually a sign that the worst will soon be over. Think of the parting of the Red Sea in the Bible and imagine an individual who is flooded with debt. The only way the Red Sea can be parted may be to declare bankruptcy. Having no credit at all might seem like a disaster, but in reality it is a corrective measure that also readjusts your perceptions about how much money you really require every month.

Another cosmic law that applies to finances is that if you face your fear head on, the burden falls away of its own weight. This can be compared to the story of Daniel, who was forced to stick his head inside the lion's mouth. The principle is that fear usually creates the block to your path in the first place. The opposite emotions of fear, confidence and courage, can remove the obstacle from your pathway.

This kind of confidence is found when your heart is aligned with your will, allowing your subconscious to be married to your spirit so that you can dispel the illusions that often accompany material hardship.

Facing your fears is a demonstration of faith that is greatly smiled upon by the Universe. If you find yourself in a difficult situation, remember that it is a good sign, as "it is always darkest before the dawn." Your matters are about to be righted and restored to karmic correctness.

It is important to realize that the cycle of supply and demand is relentlessly being exchanged. The day you die, there will probably still be a stack of bills sitting on your desk waiting to be paid. Accepting the fact that the circulation of money is a necessary part of existence is an effective way to relieve anxiety about the matter. You must be receptive to the belief that no matter how bad things get, there will always be a solution. This is a matter of faith, not only in yourself, but also in your Higher Self, which is constantly working to put you on the path to utopia.

Blessing the Money You Spend

A young girl opens a birthday card from her grandmother. Inside the card is a crisp $100 bill along with sincere wishes and hopes for happiness. A successful store rewards customers who spend more than $20 with a bonus service or gift. A woman I know writes hearts on her checks and blesses her creditors each time she makes a payment on a loan.

These individuals don't realize that they are practicing a classic cosmic law of prosperity as well as blessing others with their good wishes. The young girl's confidence is increased and the $100 brings her hundreds of more dollars as she gets her first job. The store experiences increased business as customers remember the kind gesture and return to re-experience the friendly vibration represented by the initial bonus or gift. The woman I know is unable to make her loan payment on time, yet mysteriously, the payment is held for her without penalty.

The types of actions described above demonstrate Money Magic at its highest level. Most people think a money spell is about receiving money; however, you can also spread blessings that increase your own good fortune by attaching and focusing a magical energy to the money you send out.

The key to this law of prosperity is to bless rather than resent the money you have to pay others. The goal is to see money as energy as opposed to a tangible object. One practice in magic is to gather, build and then release energy to achieve a particular purpose. That is why businesses often display the first few dollars that they earn above the cash register. This money represents good luck.

It is no coincidence that we call the coins jingling in our pockets "change," as money can be used to effect positives changes in our lives. However, our subconscious perceptions of money can stop us from becoming rich. Instinctively or subconsciously, we may resent the money we must give to others. But money that is sent out with thoughts of resentment, anxiety or desperation tends to draw more resentful, anxious or desperate situations to the sender.

Although it is a spiritual sin to worship, covet or hoard money as an object, money itself is still a sacred energy with a spiritual status. Since money involves an exchange of energy, it is considered part of the Divine Circulation and a way of circulating blessings.

To create this kind of money magic, make the monthly "pain" of paying your bills a ritual. Every time you pay your mortgage, see it as a blessing on your home. Treat your taxes as a blessing on all those who use the services that are created with that money. Sometimes I even kiss a bill after I pay it; it sounds ridiculous, but it helps change the energy associated with paying bills from negative to positive.

Spiritual law dictates that whatever you send out returns to you three times or even ten times over. Instead of performing spells in order to get money, try seeing the money you spend as a blessing for others. And if you do perform a money ritual or candle burning, at the end of the spell make a wish that others on the planet who are in need of increased prosperity will have their needs looked after as well.

Here is a general affirmation for prosperity:

"All that I touch turns to gold and green, I am a magnet drawing prosperity. As my prosperity increases so does the prosperity of all those that I pay. I pray for the best for all those I pay. Money circulates freely in my life. I shall never be weary of doing the right thing, for when I least expect it I shall reap my rewards."

What's Luck Got to Do With it?

Why is it that some people seem to be born with horseshoes up the wazoo while others battle an endless string of setbacks? Are some people born under a lucky star? Is it karma or a curse? While some are eternal victims of Murphy's Law ("if something can go wrong, it will"), others seem to get away with murder and suffer no consequences at all.

British researcher Richard Wiseman has been studying extremely lucky and unlucky people for the past ten years. The goal of his research is to discover if it is possible for anybody to become luckier.

Wiseman asked hundreds of people who felt they were either very lucky or very unlucky to fill out diaries and take part in questionnaires, IQ tests and experiments. The findings revealed that although unlucky people have almost no insight into the causes of their good and bad luck, their thoughts and behavior are responsible for much of their malfortune.

Wiseman refers to what is called the "chance opportunity" or "lucky break." We all know that lucky people consistently encounter these opportunites, while unlucky people do not. Wiseman conducted a test in which he asked both fortunate and unfortunate people to search through a newspaper and count how many photographs were inside.

On average, the unlucky people took about two minutes to count the photographs while the lucky people took just seconds. Why? Because the second page of the newspaper contained the message: "Stop counting. There are forty-three photographs in this newspaper!" This message took up half the page and was written in type that was more than two inches high. It was staring everyone in the face, but the unlucky people tended to miss it while the lucky ones tended to spot it. For fun, Wiseman apparently placed a second message halfway through the newspaper: "Stop counting. Tell the experimenter you have seen this and win seven hundred pounds." Again, the unlucky people missed the opportunity because they were still stuck in the past—too busy looking for the original forty-three photographs.

It appears that being too attached to pursuing one goal tends to make us blind to luck and opportunity. It is an experience akin to "not seeing the forest for the trees."

Wiseman's personality tests have also revealed that unlucky people are generally more tense than lucky ones, and his research has shown that anxiety disrupts people's ability to notice the unexpected. The harder the people look, the less they see.

Wiseman opened a "luck school," conducted all kinds of experiments and in the end concluded that lucky people generate good fortune by using the following three techniques:

Intuition. Unlucky people often fail to follow their intuition when making a choice, whereas lucky people tend to respect hunches. Lucky people are interested in how they think and feel about various options, rather than simply in the rational side of the situation. Gut feelings act as an alarm when making a careful decision.

Variety. Unlucky people tend to be creatures of routine. By contrast, lucky people try to introduce variety into their lives. Doing the same thing every day, or thinking about the same thing every day creates a rut that prevents people from encountering opportunity.

Positivity. Lucky people tend to see the positive side of ill fortune. When one of Wiseman's extremely lucky subjects broke his leg, he cheerfully explained that it could have been worse – he could have broken his neck.

Luck, it seems, is more of a perceptual problem than a harsh blow from fate.

So, in a nutshell, how do you change your luck? Think outside the box, think positive, don't dwell on the past, and if you fall off your horse, get right back on it. According to Wiseman, good or ill fortune is not karma, magic or a curse. Good and bad luck are is self-created. By neglecting to alter your perceptions, you may simply be cursing yourself. Never wish for yourself what you wouldn't wish for another and vice versa. Recall the old saying: "Curses have a habit of coming home to roost."

Practicing an Attitude of Gratitude

Financial favors tend to be bestowed on those who are grateful for their fortune or misfortune. Part of spiritual sophistication is taking responsibility for your actions.

When people find themselves in a difficult financial situation, most of them tend to blame everything but themselves. Although I do not recommend setting up an imaginary inner critic who constantly berates you for your mistakes, it is very important to forgive yourself and others for the mistakes that may have led you into a bad situation.

There are several ways to practice an attitude of gratitude even if you are going through the most trying of situations.

If you are experiencing a financial drought, then the best thing you can tell yourself is that "This too shall pass." You might even consider thanking the cosmos for presenting you with this situation, as it is frequently an opportunity to correct your karma or make amends.

Remember to bless your bills and the recipients of your money and practice tithing as a way of thanking the Universe for your own prosperity.

Most of us pray when we are desperate to have a request answered, but like ungrateful children, we rarely remember to thank God once the problem is relieved. There is no better time to honor your Gods then after you have been the recipient of manna from heaven.

Chapter Two

The Bank of the Higher Self

At the Bank of the Higher Self you receive more credit for smiling at a stranger than for pulling off a political coup at the office. Opening an account at the Bank of the Higher Self means improving your spiritual values so that the circulation of blessings improves the economy of the world itself.

At this bank, the more you give, the more you receive. If you have no money to give, then give instruction. If you have no instruction to give, then give positive thoughts. A smile doesn't cost a cent. The great mystic and metaphysician Paramahansa Yogananda calls these kinds of investors "smile millionaires."

Smile millionaires are investing in the foundations of prosperity, which are health, freedom, happiness and love. They have faith that every good deed will be multiplied ten-fold. They are never lenders or borrowers, because only gifts exist in this system of banking. These smile millionaires can give freely because they know that a Universe that has a supply for every demand will always meet their needs. Investors at the Bank of the Higher Self know no fear or anxiety. They do not live in the past or the future, because they know that their needs will somehow be taken care of every day.

Those who engage in uplifting, encouraging activities, who forget about the self and help others are never poor in spirit. Those who are never poor in spirit also never seem to be affected by a lack of cash. If there is lack of cash, there will be barter. If there is a lack of barter, there will be kindness, mercy and forgiveness.

Opening your own personal account at the Bank of

The Higher Self requires nothing more than faith in yourself, in the goodness and humanity of other people, and in the knowledge that what goes down must come up and vice versa.

One way to fight the lower vibrations associated with money struggles is to supply others with the very thing you think you lack. If you feel oppressed by others and think that people are not showing you kindness or mercy, then show these qualities and supply them to people in return. This is a sure way to aggregate the health, freedom, happiness and love that you deserve in life. Practicing kindness and mercy also optimizes your own vibration so that you attract only good things in life.

The cosmos rewards smile millionaires by showering them with blessings when they least expect them. The most spiritually sophisticated individuals often become rich by accident because they acknowledge that cash is only a tool that mirrors a spiritual state. The phrase "cash is king" is meaningless to these individuals because cash is not a goal. It is merely an expression of the true prosperity that occurs when they detach from desire, negate unpleasant or anxious thoughts and practice an attitude of perpetual optimism.

Whenever you have a problem, bring it to your Higher Self. Offer the burden up to this expert economist and ask this perfect you to take care of it. Stop worrying about it and within a few days, the problem will be solved.

The Laws of Karma

Karma is Sanskrit for the term "payback." The definition of karma, in a nutshell, is in the Bible: "Whatever a man soweth, so he shall reap."

If you wish prosperity for yourself, then you should

never wish poverty or sickness on another. This is a fine way to curse yourself. The sad thing about this hall of mirrors is that people often think they are being cursed by the bad energy from the very person they have been bad-mouthing.

There is power in words, so you need to be careful how you discuss and label problematic situations. However, the one thing we can learn from criticizing others is that we often tend to despise in others what we dislike about ourselves. The next time you feel the urge to criticize someone, try to see if you suffer from that same flaw and attempt to correct it.

We should also try to ask only for things that belong to us by Divine Right. Coveting what someone else has simply creates more awareness of lack in our lives. As Sinead O'Connor says "I do not want what I haven't got."

Many people believe that karma is a punishment from previous lives that must be lived out, like a pre-programmed fate. This is another good way to curse yourself by installing a negative belief in your subconscious. Transcending your karma is the entire purpose of most Eastern religions and that also means transcending the belief that you are doomed because of your karma. If anything, you are blessed every time your karma presents you with an obstacle because you are being taught not to repeat your mistakes twice.

Moreover, karma is not always responsible for our mistakes. Sometimes we simply make bad judgment calls which have bad consequences. If you don't have enough money to pay bills, it may not be the result of karma, or God punishing you. It may simply mean that you shouldn't have bought an expensive pair of shoes when you knew you had to pay the rent.

If you want to improve your payback from the universe, then it is time to reconsider what you are investing in in the first place. Are you investing pride, jealousy and ego and expecting tenderness, kindness and respect in return? Invest in those virtues that you want to multiply.

If you feel that you suffer from bad karma, the obvious thing to do is examine the garden of your soul. What kind of seeds are you sowing? What kind of finished product do you want to harvest? What kind of nutrients or support do you need to cultivate these things? It amazes me how many people sow no seeds and then expect prosperity to magically manifest itself in their lives. Good karma is a garden that is watered with virtues and where we give careful attentiveness to the thoughts we think and the words we say.

Anxiety, fear and obsession can also serve to disrupt your karma. Many people have a bad habit of getting in their own way. They will set a glorious plan in motion and then stop it from proceeding by attaching anxiety to it. They worry about the outcome until the intensity of their fear burns the life out of the project. By constantly interfering and fussing about the matter, they interfere with the circulation of positive energy. This is the equivalent of planting a seed and then constantly digging it up to see if it is still growing. Part of understanding karma is understanding the Great Wheel of Time and how it takes patience to give positive things a chance to grow. This metaphor is also true of any positive impressions that you are trying to plant in the mysterious dark silt of your subconscious. Simply plant the seed and be done with it. Have the faith that if something is meant to be it will be and if not, then it was probably bad for you. This is called practicing "the law of non-resistance." Fussing about your karma is just another modern state of neurosis.

People think that by practicing the law of non-resistance they can eliminate all karma. But there is no karma without conflict. By giving in to our fate and resigning ourselves to the idea that the Higher Powers have a grand plan for each of us to follow, all karma, good and bad, disappears instantly. You are given a clean slate on which to create impressions that will prescribe a brighter, more virtuous and prosperous future.

The Personality Versus The Higher Self

Few people achieve enlightenment in one lifetime, as both the conscious and subcoscious mind are resistant to suggestions from the Higher Self. This is because messages from the Higher Self manifest mostly as hunches and the "orders" are then perceived by the conscious mind to be irrational. However, if you operate in the belief that we live in a universe where there is a supply for every demand, then in theory nothing is impossible to attain. When in a hopeless situation, I find that repeating the mantra "With God all things are possible. Spirit is never too late!" helps.

The conscious mind is absorbed with the self. It is the self that is responsible for creating blocks to prosperity. Most prosperity blocks are created by the personality. The personality's resistance to the calls of the Higher Self are represented in the following phrases:

"I am not good enough." This is a common statement from a personality that suffers from low self-esteem. In this case, an inner critic is present, and has been probably since childhood, insisting that the individual is paid what he or she is worth: next to nothing.

"What if I fail?" This is a terrible block because it persuades the subconscious mind to attach fear to success. This kind of personality requires approval from others and is constantly weaving something that sabotages the best of plans. This kind of person is always jumping for the brass ring, and missing it by half an inch.

"There is not enough time." Your Higher Self loves truths such as "the Universe is unfolding as it should." But the personality is impatient. This kind of person feels overwhelmed and neglects to put plans in effect because he or she doesn't have the ability to make time to plan for his or her goals. These individuals often encounter a prosperity block that takes the form of a treadmill and forces them to live from paycheck to paycheck.

Another common block to prosperity is habit. Many people have been raised to feel guilty if they supercede the success of family and friends. For many, it is safer and more secure to stay at a certain income level rather than to try to become rich. Fear and guilt prevent these individuals from realizing their full potential, as they subconsciously believe that success will lead to loneliness.

Removing prosperity blocks is not easy and requires a long talk between your Higher Self and your personality. You can do this in a meditation by visualizing your perfect you (your Higher Self) having a conversation with your personality. Let your personality express its fears and see what your Higher Self has to say about the matter. This is one way to create greater self-awareness as well as recognize chronic habits that may be depriving you of money.

Casting the Burden

The best way to make financial choices and decisions is with a mind that is clear of all emotions. Messages from the Higher Self are not usually attached to any kind of heady, compulsive or emotional feeling. In fact, a feeling of elation might be a warning that your judgment is off the mark and may be the product of disturbed brain chemistry.

When you are in dire financial straits and at an absolute loss as to what to do, you might want to try a sincere prayer. As Lisa Simpson once said, "Prayer is the last refuge of rascals and scoundrels."

The most common way to release a burden is to cast it up to God or a Higher Power. Some people refer to this as "giving it to the Universe." The prayer is usually worded something like this:

"Please God, this is too much for me. Whether I am naughty or nice, I am still your child and I ask to be taken care of. Please help me to resolve this situation, but if it can't be resolved then help me to accept it. If there is loss, than please replace it with an equivalent or better gain. Amen."

You might also want to try Elizabeth Clare Prophet's Violet Flame ritual. According to this great visionary metaphysician's spiritual practice, the Violet Flame is a metaphor for the ability of the Higher Self to erase problems. The ritual is a way of casting the burden of your problems onto the Universe to be taken care of. I usually light a violet candle and picture all my burdens, anxieties and resentments being transformed into positive energy by the power of the flame. This lovely ritual greatly relieves stress and helps bypass the personality in order to access the inspiration and wisdom of the Higher Self. Its most therapeutic aspect is its intention to practice transmutation: all negative energy is transformed into positive manifestations through the power of the Divine Light.

Chapter Three

The Power of the Spoken Word

Life and death reside in the power of the spoken word. This is why we are encouraged to pray aloud. Vocalizing a request is believed to manifest it into reality. The human voice has a vibration that is believed to work on the astral plane.

Many people use their personality to manifest events instead of relying on the power of God or the Higher Self. The Higher Self dwells in your super-conscious, which is a place of illumination, inspiration and trust. A person with a rich consciousness attracts riches. A person with a poor consciousness attracts poverty.

The best way to contact your Higher Self or God is through simple prayer spoken out loud.

Prayers work best when you wish for the best possible outcome of a situation, rather than a specific outcome. When in doubt, ask for the situation to be resolved in the best way possible for yourself and for others.

Be Careful What You Wish For

I have always been fascinated by the concept of wishing, especially "collective wishing." If enough people wish for the same thing, does it make it happen? For instance, humans probably always wished they could talk to each other without requiring physical contact. Perhaps the invention of the telephone was the result of a long-standing collective wish from caveman days. From the long perspective of human history, the telephone, which literally manifests distant voices into thin air, truly is a magical object.

If you are going to wish for money, make your wish

as simple as possible. The wish can be a short prayer or request to the Heavens above.

There are some cosmic laws that rule the concept of wishing.

The first rule is not to wish too hard for something. Wishing too hard or too often creates a rebound effect. The Universe does not like an imbalance and it may perceive the emotion, desire or desperation you are attaching to the wish as a kind of "shove" that throws others out of astral balance. For instance, if you ask to be promoted, but that promotion takes a job away from another person, you could find your own job disappearing. The idea behind this concept is that every person has his or her own guardian angel that protects him or her from other people's bad wishes.

Negative wishes inspired by an emotion like jealousy don't work well. Wishing that your ex-husband's girlfriend was out of the picture so that you could receive more child support is a wish that is not likely to be fulfilled. You are better off rephrasing the wish: "I wish for the highest good for my children."

When it comes to wishing, sometimes it is better to wish for the essence of a thing, rather than the thing itself. For instance, wishing for a certain sum of cash might bring you just that sum of cash and nothing else.

Anxiety and fear cannot be attached to wishes granted in realms that are ruled by spirits, angels and fairies. These beings are said to be repelled by wishes that have selfish motivations. Making a negative wish can function like a curse.

Much of the crap brought upon civilization is the result of collective negative wishing. Consider John F. Kennedy Junior's plane crash a few years ago. For generations, people have been aware of the so-called

Kennedy curse. Was it the mass belief in this curse, a form of negative wishing in itself, that brought down JFK's plane? Is it something that we all, subconsciously, thought should happen?

Prayers and wishes are strengthened when they are the result of group desire and good intentions. However, getting someone else to pray with you or support your request in a prayer circle can be risky business as the person might be praying for what he or she thinks is best for you as opposed to your highest good.

Another principle of wishing is "wishing overkill." Wishes come true if they function like a nudge—done in a simple way, and from the heart. If you are able to gently nudge the Universe with your thoughts, you're in luck. You have to be part of the universal state of harmony. If you interrupt this balance with an explosion of determinism, selfishness or passion, then you often experience a boomerang and see the opposite result come into effect. This is similar to witchcraft's 3x3x3 rule: whatever you send out comes back to you. It also explains the persistence of Murphy's Law.

Another important principle that involves both the practice of prayer and wishing is the principle of "like attracts like." If you are in a state of anxiety and wish for "more serenity," you are likely to find yourself surrounded by anxious people also wishing for serenity. Stating that you lack something actually reinforces its lack. Combine this with the principle of resonance where a wish is reinforced by the number of people thinking the same thing, and it really makes you realize that group negative wishing may actually be responsible for many of the ills in the world.

The next time you make a wish, wish well. Wish for the best results for all concerned and don't be attached to the outcome. When you wish upon a star, it DOES make a difference who you are...

Writing Letters to God

Those who are not familiar with prayer or who have trouble connecting to their Higher Selves through speaking out loud may want to try keeping what is called A Day and Night Journal.

Below I have developed a simple journal program that will help to guide you and strengthen your faith in yourself and in your ability to handle the future.

First of all, buy yourself a notebook that you really like and that has a hard enough cover that you can write sitting up in bed. Keep this journal by your bedside because you will write in it every day for at least ten minutes, once in the morning and once at night. In this book you will have your own personal conversations with God. It is an incredibly efficient way to clear any prosperity blocks that may be encouraged by your personality as it resists following your Higher Path.

As soon as you wake up in the morning, open your journal and, for ten minutes, write down everything that comes to mind. This is not a "to do" list although many of you will find yourself writing all kinds of things. I address my journal directly to God. I start each chapter with "Dear God, Ascended Masters, Angels and Good Fairies." Then I start writing exactly what is on my mind. For example: "Dear God, today I really need help with my car. It's broken down and I don't know how I am going to pay for the new brakes, but please help me find a source of money. Also, my friend Sally has not called me for a couple of days. Could you please reveal to me what is going on? And this morning I woke up really hating everything. Could you please help me with that..." and so on. Don't worry about spelling, just let the words flow. When you do this you release all the resentment and anxiety that may be blocking you from efficiently continuing with your day. You are also giving the problems up to a Higher Source and asking that power to provide you with a solution. When you have done this, list five things in your life that you are truly grateful for and thank God for them on paper. It does not matter if the things you are grateful for are big or small. "Thank you for the great sandwich I had at lunch today. Thank you for the insurance check. Thank you for my beautiful pet. Thank you for the smile from the bank teller yesterday."

Then go about your day. You will be amazed at how much smoother things run and how solutions to your little problems seem to miraculously appear. I think this is because the writing discipline resembles the discipline of prayer and the cosmos smiles on both.

Before you go to bed do the same thing. First of all thank God for how He/She has helped you that day, or question Him/Her if certain problems still persist. I find it helps to write something like, "God, please take this problem away, get rid of it. I can't handle it. Either that or help me find a way to make it better or accept the situation." Then do what you did in the morning by pouring out questions and concerns on paper. You can also list five people who have wronged you and ask for the strength to forgive them. After that, think of another five things you are grateful for and then list TEN people you know and ask God to give them blessings or provide solutions to their problems. For example: "Jenny next door is having a hard time making ends meet and taking care of those kids. Please bless her and help her meet her needs so she can do better."

This is not as much work as it seems, and it is amazing how writing in a journal for ten minutes in the morning and at night, can help you balance your emotions, achieve clarity and manifest little miracles in your life. When you look back on your journal, you will be astounded by the number of requests that have been filled, and by the way things you used to find upsetting are not a source of pain anymore. You don't have to be a great writer to do this. God doesn't care about grammar or fancy penmanship. Just write from your heart.

Positive Affirmations

Positive affirmations are another form of prayer. Their purpose is to use the spoken word to mold or make an impression on the subconscious mind. This encourages the manifestation of positive events in your life.

How can you be "better, instead of bitter" when life hands you what feels like a terrible blow, whether to your heart, pocketbook or soul?

First of all, it is important to remember that you are not alone. Nobody gets through life unscathed. Everyone must face disease, death, poverty, abandonment or heartbreak. However, as the old saying goes, "It is not the cards you have been dealt, but how you play them that counts." (And I don't mean Tarot cards here, either!)

Apparently, the unpleasant experiences that we attract into our lives are the result of a lack of faith in the Higher Power that lives within each and every one of us. This lack of faith manifests itself in a desire to control or a reluctance to let go. Dwelling on the past (especially to happier times) is also a big block, as it creates a feeling of discontent that prevents you from connecting with the wisdom of your inner self.

This is why it is important for each and every one of

us to practice some form of positive thinking and to replace all negative thoughts with thoughts of forgiveness, hope and success, no matter how hard it is. I know I cringe whenever I think about this, because my personality does NOT want to do it, but one of the best ways to ensure future success is to forgive or bless the person who has hurt you the most.

If you want to be rich, in spirit or otherwise, you have to recognize that whatever you think, especially if it is negative, comes back to you in one form or another. For example, if you wish hellfire on an ex-boyfriend's head, you might experience that yourself in another form. For instance, it is a common belief amongst alternative health practitioners and neurolinguistic programmers that resentment causes cancer. As a psychic, I see this principle of "like attracts like" in action all the time. The metaphor commonly used to describe how words and expressions can be used to carve out your future is the unhewn block of marble. You are the artist and your words and thoughts determine whether you see an angel or a devil in the uncut marble. It is important to train your mind so that it sees the future as a blank slate. If you see nothing but demons when you look at a blank page, you will literally write yourself a disaster script or carve a demon out of the marble, attracting the next bad job or boyfriend.

You can choose several affirmations and write them down every night. I recommend choosing ten and sticking with them till things are right or you can choose shorter affirmations and recite them to yourself. Peruse the list below and use the ones that feel right to you.

Infinite Spirit, please bring to me what is mine, at the right time, and in the right way.

I am increasingly magnetic to money, prosperity and abundance. I create what I want through energy that is guided by the Divine Imagination.

The Universe is my unfailing supply, and large sums of money come to me at the right time under perfect grace and in perfect ways. Spirit is never too late!

I cannot lose that which is mine by Divine Right. If I do then it is replaced by its equivalent or better.

Divine Love, through me, now dissolves all obstacles, and my highest good flows to me in a steady, unbroken and increasing stream of prosperity. My happiness is between God and me.

Unexpected opportunities present themselves, unexpected paths to prosperity open, and endless avalanches of abundance are given to me under grace and in perfect ways.

As I am made in God's image, and His power is limitless, my own power to create a prosperous future is limitless as well. Infinite intelligence guides me and solves every problem.

My reality is a reality of plenty, and I now receive all that I desire or require and much more.

I spend money wisely and with confidence, knowing the Universe has a supply for every demand.

Divine Imagination inspires my right actions. I now let go of worn out conditions and bad habits. Divine Order is established in every corner of my mind, body and financial affairs. My seemingly impossible good now happens.

There is no competition on the spiritual plane. What God has done for others, He can do for me!

My endless good now comes to me in endless ways. I am harmonious, poised and magnetic. I now draw to myself my own. My power is God's power and is irresistible. I see clearly, act quickly and my greatest expectations come to pass in a miraculous way.

I cast this burden on the Christ Within (God, the Higher Self or the Violet Flame) and I go free!

I expect only the best to happen and it does.
I am prosperous in all areas of my life.
I expect profitable surprises.
I circulate what I have.
My honesty brings me good fortune.
Doing what I love serves others.
I now accept my rightful abundance.
I am ready and willing to change.
I connect with my inner power and expand my ability to receive.
I live in the present.
There is no such thing a debt in the Divine Mind.
I have an attitude of gratitude.
I take responsibility for making my own changes.
I am ready to accept wealth.
I easily dissolve limiting beliefs.
I trust my Higher Self.
There is good in everything that happens to me from now on.

I believe in my unlimited potential.
I rejoice in the good fortune of others.
I choose thoughts that support a prosperous future.
I am creating a new life.
I am aware of my Higher Self as the true source of prosperity.
I transcend the laws of karma through right action.
The universe has a supply for every demand.
Time presents me with the perfect answers.
I always put my goals in writing.
I fuel my dreams with faith.

How to Write Your Own Affirmation

You don't have to use pre-written affirmations. You can tailor your affirmation to suit your situation. However, if you create your own affirmations there are several guidelines to follow, especially if you have asked for a specific request.

For example, let's say that I am in immediate need of $20,000. I would say,

"I, Samantha, immediately receive $20,000 dollars and more. I also ask that all those in immediate financial need receive money so that prosperity is circulated freely among all. I give thanks for all of the blessings I have received in the past and those that I am about to receive."

There are a few things you might want to notice about how the above statement is worded.

First of all, your name along with the word "I" is written into the affirmation so that the subconscious makes no mistake about who the money is intended for. The word "immediately" is used to express the idea that what is about to happen has already happened. Since the phrase is written to express a specific request (not usually recommended), be sure to leave a loophole. The loophole in the above affirmation is $20,000 or more. The affirmation includes a request that all those in financial need receive it. Finally, the statement expresses an attitude of gratitude.

In my experience, an affirmation that is made for a specific request is sometimes not as effective as a more general affirmation, although some affirmation writers would disagree. Here is an example of the first line of a non-specific affirmation:

"I, Samantha, immediately receive all the money that I need at the right time, in the right place and under the auspices of Divine Grace."

You can also make a request list and create one master affirmation that you write down for several days. Here is an example of a master affirmation:

I, (your name), DESERVE TO BE AND NOW AM happy. My life is rich, rewarding and full of fun and pleasure. I live in the present. Any negative unwanted thoughts and fears have left or are leaving my body and I am beautiful, vibrant and healthy. I am calm, peaceful and look forward to the future. I thank (God or Higher Power) every day for all my blessings and fully accept even those blessings that seem to be in disguise. I enjoy abundance and success. I am free from fear and disease and I trust that I will be safe. I have choices, and can handle anything that comes my way. I do not desire anything because I am perfect as I am now. I am the perfect manifestation of God's divine plan for my life. I forgive all those who have hurt me and I wish the same blessings for all that I do for myself. I accept this done in this hour in full power according to the Divine Will of God."

Prayers for Prosperity

The psalms of the Bible are a literary treasure chest of prayers for prosperity. Below is a list of Psalms to recite for common financial requests. In some Catholic and Santeria traditions, the prayer is spoken or written out after lighting a candle. You may also recite the prayer as many times as you want to transform it into a kind of a mantra.

Psalm 3: To conquer fear of poverty.

Psalm 5: To ask for a special financial favour.

Psalm 6: To ask for mercy from creditors.

Psalm 8: To improve confidence and bring customers to a business.

Psalm 14: To renew faith that the universe is unfolding as it should.

Psalm 19: To receive daily blessings and increase faith in the idea that the universe has a supply for every demand.

Psalm 21: To increase your spiritual vibration so as to invite prosperity into your life.

Psalm 22: For deliverance from difficult financial situations, when you feel hopeless or backed into a corner.

Psalm 23: For serenity, peace of mind and stillness of the spirit, and to help access the Higher Self.

Psalm 30: For patience and acceptance of Divine Will, and to understand that time brings what we need when appropriate.

Psalm 33: When feeling fearful.

Psalm 38: For protection in court.

Psalm 44: For mercy when you find yourself in an intolerable or unjust situation; to strengthen faith in God.

Psalm 45: To increase your faith in the power of the subconscious to follow your stated words.

Psalm 47: To reinforce the four cornerstones of prosperity: health, freedom, happiness and love.

Psalm 48: To become a "smile millionaire" by reinforcing happiness and faith.

Psalm 49: To overcome envy of the prosperity of others.

Psalm 54: To master doubts and negative thoughts.

Psalm 64: To increase confidence, decrease fears of hidden enemies and to ask to be in the right place at the right time.

Psalm 65: To give thanks for blessings that you have received.

Psalm 66: To give thanks for an answered prayer.

Psalm 67: To give thanks for what you have, and to eliminate discontent.

Psalm 69: For deliverance in times of suffering.

Psalm 70: To repel the negative thoughts and attitudes of others.

Psalm 71: For liberation from limiting thoughts or situations that seem like a trap and to encourage confidence and persistence.

Psalm 73: To eliminate feelings of anger, jealousy and resentment that take away opportunities for your own enrichment.

Psalm 74: To attract good fortune and repel enemies.

Psalm 75: To encourage a hiring or a job promotion.

Psalm 76: Traditionally, for winning the lottery or luck at gambling.

Psalm 84: To develop a more optimistic view of the future and attract prosperity.

Psalm 87: To promote success in the arts (read this affirmation out loud before an audition, interview, exhibition or pitching session).

Psalm 99: For mercy in legal proceedings.

Psalm 100: To repel negative energy and harmful influences.

Psalm 101: To break bad habits such as overspending.

Psalm 102: To receive an answer to a specific problem.

Psalm 103: To engage your willingness to change for the better, and for stillness and grace.

Psalm 108: For success in business.

Psalm 111: To find the right job or career path.

Psalm 113: To receive applause, awards or accolades.

Psalm 115: To resist naysayers and uncooperative people.

Psalm 123: To assure the free circulation of kindness as energy in your life.

Psalm 126: To understand that problems are temporary and that this too shall pass.

Psalm 129: For deliverance against financial oppression.

Psalm 132: To acquire material goods and property.

Psalm 135: To strengthen the heart and will so that you are led to your highest aspirations in life.

Psalm 139: To instill confidence in God and the Divine Plan that is in store for you, or when you feel lost, confused or sad.

Psalm 141: To receive answers for specific financial requests, and for confidence and peace of mind.

Psalm 143: To restore faith in your path and renew confidence that there will be a joyful, hopeful tomorrow.

Psalm 147: For a peaceful heart during times of turmoil.

Psalm 150: To obtain blessings and express gratitude for those blessings.

A simple prayer:
"Dear Lord, guide me to honor you with my talents and treasures. Amen."

Chapter Four

CREATIVE MANIFESTATION
The Power of Visualization

Visualization is not so much about magic as it is about seeing a goal. A man or woman's potential is only as limited as the reach of his or her imagination. If you picture small things, you will get small things. If you picture your future as having too many possibilities, you will always be indecisive. If you picture the best, you will get the best.

Visualizations work in much the same way as positive affirmations. Most of us have the bad habit of picturing the worst case scenario as our thoughts are assaulted with worry, negativity and "what if's." Most of us start out picturing how we want our day to proceed, but by the end of the day this picture becomes blurred as we absorb doubts and fears from television, newspapers and other people.

The key to manifesting prosperity through creative visualization is to learn how to suspend an image in your mind by depositing it in your subconscious after you have pictured the desired goal. In order for a creative visualization to work you must use your imagination to picture the outcome in as much detail as possible.

For instance, let's say you need to find a new apartment. The first thing you need to do is to empty your head as much as possible of all thoughts so that your mind is like a blank slate.

You might want to assist your imagination by asking yourself a number of questions about the ideal apartment. How big is it? How much is the rent? Does it have high ceilings? Visualize the layout and every detail of the apartment as accurately as you can and continuing to layer on these elements. Walk through your imaginary apartment. What do you see when you look out the window? Do you see an urban wasteland or a leafy park? The more detail you can conjure, the more likely you are to manifest the apartment that is right for you.

Visualize more than you expect. For instance, if you know that the apartment you are thinking of is in the range of $1400 a month, but you can only afford $800, don't tell yourself that your dream apartment is not possible. Keep picturing it exactly as you want it, and at the price you can afford.

Once you have visualized the apartment and are satisfied with every detail, picture yourself depositing the image into the treasure box of your subconscious. Tell yourself the apartment will be yours, and then ask the Universe to make it so. It is absolutely amazing how, through this technique, many people manage to find the supply that meets their demand.

Treasure Maps

Some people are not visually oriented and find it a challenge to use their imagination or focus their mind on a goal.

One way to get around this problem is to make what is called a treasure map or treasure book. This involves collecting images and pasting them onto a backing to form a collage.

The artistic process of collaging is similar to the layering process used in creative visualization—you are continually adding desired elements to the "big picture."

For instance, to make a treasure map or treasure book to find an apartment, start cutting out images of houses, yards, apartments, furniture and swatches of favorite colors and start pasting them onto paper or cardboard. Good sources of images are catalogues and magazines. The images function as symbols that are impressed upon the subconscious and serve to fill in any details that the imagination has failed to supply.

The idea is that you are trying to create synchronicity by finding symbolic images of what you want in your future. For instance, if you are fed up with apartments that have small ugly bathrooms, cut out pictures of large bathrooms that have gleaming counters, designer fixtures and shiny tiles.

You can create a treasure map or treasure book in a day or two, or over a period of weeks, by constantly adding more images. If you have no idea how to begin, one suggestion is to lay the first image down in the center of the paper and paste the images in a clockwise spiral. The spiral creates a vortex shape that draws the desired energies towards you.

The Power of Vocalization

For centuries, the power of the human voice has been used as a tool for transformation, manifestation and healing. In almost every culture, human sounds are thought to create matter from non-existence. Techniques range from emitting noise from the diaphragm to chanting, singing and group prayer.

The human diaphragm, rather than the throat, is believed to be the Third Chakra, or seat of the soul. Sustaining a single note from the Third Chakra (the energy center of the diaphragm) connects us to divine powers. The human breath sustains all life. Without control over our breath, and the notes that it sounds, we have no control over our lives. In many cultures the soul is thought to reside in the breath.

Perhaps the oldest culture known to practice vocalization is Tibetan. Different musical notes are attributed to different Chakras (or energy centers in the body). The Chakras, in fact, can be compared to piano keys with the base Chakra representing a low C, and the crown Chakra a high C. In different cultures, different musical notes are believed to attract different vibrations. For instance, Balinese temple bells are always pitched at a pure C as this note is thought to clear sacred spaces of bad energy.

Tibetan singing bowls have a similar purpose. These crystal or metal bowls are cast or carved in tune with musical notes. Sounds are made by rubbing the rim of the bowl with an implement, similar to wetting the rim of a wine glass with a finger and circling the rim to make a sound. Singing bowls are a meditative device whose original purpose was to clear energy fields, manifest the different qualities that are represented by that note and draw these qualities to the player.

Great power resides in a group of human voices chanting or singing together, which is why group vocalization is an essential component of most religious music, whether it is Gyoto monks chanting or a gospel choir singing. The magic of manifestation is believed to be in the sustaining of the notes.

The Om and the Ah

Perhaps the simplest form of prosperity meditation you can practice is the vocalization of the Om and the Ah sounds.

The Ah is one of the first sounds we make when we are born. It is also the cry of sexual ecstasy, discovery and surprise. Many cultures associate this sound with the creative element of the breath that is used to manifest miracles. The Ah sound is used to open the diaphragm, remove blocks and increase the powers of the imagination.

The Om sound is associated with the receptive element of the imagination and is used to signify or complete the union with the Higher Self. It is a noise that expresses the faith that Higher Powers will "make it so."

Both the Ah and the Om sounds are used to open the diaphragm so that the Soul is unified with the breath. It is the outgoing breath, the exhalation, that delivers the sound that manifests matter from the non-existent.

The traditional method of using the Om and the Ah is to practice vocalizing these sounds twice a day. The Ah sound is pronounced upon waking and often while still lying in bed. The vocalization technique involves taking in the fullest breath possible from the stomach and then emitting the sound for as long as possible. With the first few Ahs, picture your mind as a clean slate. If any anxious thoughts come up, simply discard them. When you feel that your mind is clear of all anxiety, visualize what you would like to manifest for a few minutes. The optimum moment to do your visualization is at that point of stillness between the inhaled breath and the exhaled breath. You should do this exercise for at least twenty minutes in the morning for optimum effect.

The Om vocalization is usually done at night for an additional twenty minutes. Once again, clear your mind and visualize your goals, but this time, on the exhale, picture your goal as something that has already happened. In fact, the Om is a kind of "thank you" for future prosperity or an expression of certainty that what you want to happen will indeed take place. Once again, it is important to hold the Om sound for as long as possible as you exhale.

You can also use this exercise simply as a meditation to clear the mind or to receive direction from the Higher Self when there seems to be no answers. The idea is by centering yourself so that you are still enough to receive energies from higher powers, you create new inspiration and direction.

Soul Talk

Since the nature of money is to circulate, it is sometimes necessary to deal with other personalities in order to manifest prosperity.

One way to do this is to have a Soul Talk with an individual who you think may be of some assistance. A soul talk is particularly valuable after a job interview or when negotiating with individuals you don't like, such as creditors or tax collectors.

The intention of a Soul Talk is to try to correct a situation that is Divine in nature.

The simplest form of a Soul Talk is to actually have a conversation in your mind with the other person. Begin by picturing the person's face. Even if you don't know what he or she looks like, let an image form in your mind.

First, picture what the individual looks like. Next, assess his or her vibe. How does the person "feel" to you? Do you sense resistance to you contacting him or her? Are you greeted with familiarity? What is person's posture or expression?

The next step is to imagine the individual coming towards you, smiling. This may be particularly difficult with people that you owe money to or feel are oppressing you, but it is a necessary part of the exercise. By picturing the person's smile, you are subtly increasing his or her receptivity to the message you are sending.

Once you have completely imagined the individual, picture a beam of light shooting from your heart to the other person's heart. This beam can be like a laser, a cascade of shimmering light or a long silver thread. Use whatever image feels most comfortable.

Next, picture a tiny sun several feet above your own head. This is your Soul Light or your Higher Self. Above that, picture an even higher light. The best way to imagine this supreme light is as a small ball hovering about halfway between you and the person with whom you are "soul talking." This third light represents the Divine, or the holiness that connects all Souls. This is the Highest Sun, the source of all creativity, imagination and manifestation.

The next step is to picture the Highest Sun sending a beam to your Soul Light and down to your Heart Light. Many people feel a warm glow around their chest when they do this correctly. However, if you don't feel this, don't worry. Often it is enough just to picture the light in order for the communication to be successful.

Imagine that the person you are picturing also has a Soul Light hovering about three feet above his or her head. The Higher Sun is also sending light down to his or her Soul Light and Heart Light.

At this point, you will notice that you have created a kind of triangle between yourself and the imagined individual, with the Higher Sun Light shedding two rays that join both Soul Lights and a lateral ray connecting both Heart Lights.

You are now going to attempt to communicate with the other person Soul to Soul by sending a beam of light that will connect your Soul Lights. Many visualizers will feel a connection with the other person before reaching this part of the visualization.

Once you have connected with the individual and feel the contract between you Soul Lights, you have three choices. You can say out loud what you would like and why it would be good, send the person different colors or, use a combination of verbal communication and light emanation. Do whatever seems right to you.

Saying your thoughts out loud is a direct and simple way to make Soul contact, and attuned individuals may hear messages from the other person's Soul. The important thing is to you make your request, such as "Please consider hiring me."

Purists who perform this exercise prefer not to have a conversation but rather simply send the other individual different colors and qualities of light for a few minutes. You can picture a soft pink light and followed by a bright blue and then a green one. If you don't know what colors to send, picture a rainbow and send each color in succession.

The quality of light you send is also a factor. You can send a pearlescent light, a cascade of sparkles, an intense laser, or a pulsating beam. When conversing in light mode, be sure to also pause, and ask the individual to send you light in turn. Even though all of this is taking place in the realm of the imagination, it is amazing how often you will feel a surge of light come to you from the other person. It is through these surges that you will get an indication whether or not you are on the right path and have made the right choices.

At the end of the exercise, draw light back towards yourself in the reverse order: first from the Higher Sun, then from your Heart Light and then from your Soul Light. Picture the other person doing the same. As you part ways with the individual on the Soul Plane, be sure to smile.

The Soul Talk visualization is derived partly from light working techniques and partly from practices associated with Tibetan occultists. A quick version of the visualization can be achieved by simply picturing the individual and sending them light.

This exercise usually results in at least a phone call from the individual in question. Sometimes the person will say that he or she has been thinking of you, had a dream about you or felt compelled to reverse a bad decision.

The exercise can also be used to manifest an individual that you don't know, such as a potential employer or a mentor. Perform the exercise as usual, but do not concentrate on visualizing the details of the person's appearance. This version of the exercise is like making a "call" on the astral plane allowing just the right person to manifest in your life.

The Wheel of Light

This is a meditation that I used to perform live in the Psychic Realm chat room. I find it not only lessens worries about money, but it also has the effect of bringing what you need into manifestation. I have several versions the meditation for different purposes such as finding love, contacting ancestors or creating harmony, but the one below is designed to draw in money, prosperity and opportunity.

The Wheel of Light is what is described as an open call on the astral plane to Souls who can assist you with financial and career matters. You are not making any kind of specific request in this meditation, and you are not picturing individuals. You are asking for what belongs to you to be brought to you by Divine Right.

Before you begin the meditation it is important to be in a relaxed position, either sitting up or lying down in a quiet place where you will not be disturbed. If you are sitting up, uncross your legs and put your feet flat on the floor. Close your eye and place your palms face up on your knees. Make sure your spine is straight and your shoulders relaxed. If you are lying down, keep your legs straight and lie with your palms face up.

Once you are relaxed, try taking a few deep breaths from your diaphragm. You are truly breathing from your diaphragm if your stomach rises up and sinks down, rather than to your chest.

First picture a pinpoint of light growing in the center of your abdomen. The color of this light is golden yellow. Each time you take a breath, the light expands, until it feels like it is warming your entire chest cavity with a syrupy light.

Now picture your heart center as a closed flower. Your heart center can resemble any flower; very often your subconscious determines what kind of flower is in your heart. Picture the petals of this flower slowly unfurling each time you take a breath. Keep unfolding these petals until the flower is completely open.

Inside the flower is a pinpoint of light that resembles a sparkling jewel. You may decide whether it is a diamond, a ruby or an emerald.

Now, with each exhalation picture the golden light from your stomach center, also known as the Third Chakra, sending a stream of light to your heart center. Each time you exhale, picture this light energizing and expanding the jewel in the center of your heart's blossom. Some people will experience the sensation that the petals are rotating in a clockwise fashion.

Keep energizing this jewel with breaths from your solar plexus until you feel the light within it getting larger. Some people imagine this light as golden, others as white, pink or violet. Feel this light expand and fill your entire body until each cell sparkles with light.

Next, imagine the light that is emanating from your heart expanding outside your body by at least three feet. Take it one step further and fill the room with light. Once you feel you have accomplished this, see how far you can expand the light that is coming from your heart's center. Expand it outside your home and feel it reach throughout your neighborhood and city.

You will know it is time to stop emanating light when you feel a slight click or a sense of completion. You have cleared your auric field and raised your vibration to attract positive events into your life through the power of light.

Now that you have blasted your immediate energy field with light, the next step is to close your eyes and picture a midnight blue sky. In this visualization, stars represent the souls of other individuals.

First, ask your imagination or Higher Self to fill the empty sky with the stars (Soul Lights) of all of those individuals who could help you with your career and with financial goals at the present time. You don't have to visualize faces, since it doesn't matter who these people are—the aim is to make contact with many Souls, not personalities. In fact, with this visualization, the less specific you make it, the more likely you are to meet with success.

As you ask the Divine Imagination to fill this blank sky, you will see your visual field filling with pinpoints of brilliant light. Once again, you will feel a click or experience a sense of completion once you have finished this phase.

Next, ask the Divine Imagination to fill the sky with people who have helped you with your finances and career in the past. Once again, you will see your visual field fill with additional stars. These are the Souls of all of those who have contributed to your present financial conditions.

Picture the sky filling with the Soul Lights of all of those individuals you are likely to meet in the future. This includes mentors, employers, bank employees, relatives or anyone else that can help you achieve prosperity.

Now turn your attention back to your heart's center. You are about to send light to all of the stars that you have pictured in your mental sky.

On the next exhalation, picture the jewel in your heart's center emitting an intense beam of silver light to all of the stars in your visual field. As you send out light, you will probably see these stars become brighter. Now ask these stars to send a similar quality of light back to you.

Next, send out a warm golden light as steady and soft as multiple shafts of sunlight. Send this light out to all the stars in your visual field. Once again, picture these stars sending light back. Don't worry if not every star sends you light. The reason you are sending out different colors and qualities of light is because different Souls respond to different kinds of light working at different times. What will be, will be.

Now picture a soft pink light going from your heart to the Soul Lights. With each exhalation picture this light getting stronger. Send this rosy fire to the stars and be receptive to the light that you receive back.

The next step is to imagine an intense, laser beam green light that shoots out to all the stars in your visual field. Imagine this green light turning to gold and then change its quality so that it shimmers. After you are done sending this, wait to receive light back.

If more stars appear as you do this, don't worry. This

probably means that you are manifesting more "money contacts." Whatever you do, don't try to control or censor your mind's eye.

Now send every star rays of violet and multicolored light. Start out with a strong beam and then reduce it to a twinkle. Change it back to a strong beam until you feel your message has been transmitted.

Now ask the stars to enter your heart. You can picture them zooming towards you or approaching gradually. Watch as the stars become tinier and are absorbed by the jewel in the center of your heart's blossom. Feel your heart become energized and made glad by the entrance of these souls.

Finally, when you feel that the million pinpoints of light have entered your heart's blossom, it is time to close the petals. With each exhalation, picture the petals of your heart's blossom folding over your jewel so that it once again looks like a little bud.

To close the meditation, take your right hand and place it over your heart. Place your left hand over your right hand. Utter the words "Peace be still."

Creative Visualizations

Creative Visualization involves fashioning an image in the conscious mind and charging (and constant recharging) that image with the psychic energy of the unconscious.

You can practice a Creative Visualization any time or any place. The most important thing to remember is to picture the visualization in as much detail as your imagination allows. After all, visualizations are a form of self-programming.

The results of visualization may materialize in various ways. Sometimes they manifest in a sudden and unusual manner, but mostly they manifest in a natural and gradual fashion.

Picture what you want. If you cannot "see" what you want in your mind's eye, then get a feeling for it or "write" the words on the chalkboard in your head.
You might also want to try the movie screen technique. Imagine yourself walking into a movie theater and choose a comfortable seat. Watch as the curtains roll back and a movie of your project or goal unfolds. Make sure to experience your emotions as you watch yourself in the movie. This is one way of turning a disaster script for your life into a successful script.

Unless a visualization is injected with passion and enthusiasm, it is just a daydream. Question yourself to make sure your heart is aligned with your will, as the personality is generally resistant to big changes. When you imagine having what you want, ask yourself how it makes you feel. If you don't feel joy, you are probably wishing for something that is not yours by Divine Right. Spend a few minutes enjoying your visualization several times a day. Don't sweat it. Don't try too hard. Take a few minutes and a few deep breaths and imagine. Enjoy the time you spend in this creative process. If you are not sure whether what you want is for your highest good speak these words "This or something better for the highest good of all concerned."

After you have used these three keys for creating what you want, release the picture to the Powers That Be. Thank your Higher Self and Spirit for bringing you your desire. Don't get attached to the outcome. Remember that Creative Visualization is about seeking the essence of the thing. Be prepared to be surprised with whatever comes your way.

The following is a collection of visualizations

inspired by various cultures that work in much the same way as positive affirmations. These visualizations provide the subconscious with a symbolic path to achieving prosperity.

The Prosperity Tree

Picture yourself opening your front door. At your feet is a small gold box wrapped with golden ribbon. Bring the box inside and unwrap it. Inside is a tiny golden acorn.

Go outside into the garden. The sun is shining and the flowers are blooming. Find the perfect spot to plant your acorn.

Once you are back in the house the doorbell rings. You open the door and find a bottle wrapped with pink ribbon. The bottle reads "Elixir of Love."

Take this bottle out to the garden and uncork it. It has a lovely fragrance. Pour the sparkling liquid onto the spot where you planted the golden acorn.

Suddenly life moves beneath the earth and your tree begins to grow. It grows fast and tall. It is strong and healthy and unfurls many branches, leaves and blossoms. And it is an unusual tree— every flower on it is a different species. There are orchids, roses and hybrids you have never seen before.

Soon birds come to sing in the tree. Note the different kinds of birds. Owls, nightingales, eagles and winged creatures you have never seen before suddenly arrive. Imagine that you can hear them singing.

The elixir has caused the tree to grow quickly, and now it is sprouting fruit. But as it is an unusual tree, it grows different kinds of fruit on every branch—pomegranates, apples, peaches, pineapples and other delights.

Pick a fruit from this tree and savor its fragrant flesh and juice. Consume the whole thing, even the peel and the core. Eat as many fruits as you like. Take time to enjoy this food in the visualization.

Now imagine the sun getting brighter and all the leaves of the tree turning into coins and dollar bills. As they fall to the ground, gather up this wealth in a bright green bag.

Now the tree is shedding golden acorns. Each time an acorn falls you plant it and a new tree begins a new life cycle.

Before you complete this visualization, imagine your Tree of Life sprouting new leaves and blossoms to celebrate another cycle of spring and renewal.

The Money Temple

Picture yourself at the base of a tall mountain. Your job is to climb the mountain, but the prospect seems daunting. You call to your Higher Self for help.

Your Higher Self appears - a healthier, stronger twin image of yourself. You greet your Higher Self and he or she smiles, picks you up and carries you up the mountain. At the top, your Higher Self deposits you at the front doors of a beautiful temple.

You start to knock on the door, but it is not necessary. The doors magically swings open to reveal a square courtyard filled with exotic flowers. In the center of this courtyard is a gleaming fountain. You admire the way the spray from the fountain is refracted into rainbows.

You take off your clothes and bathe in the refreshing, invigorating waters. When you are finished bathing, you discover that your old clothes have been taken away and replaced with new ones. You put on these clothes. In a pocket of these new vestments is a golden coin. You make a wish and throw the coin into the fountain as a thank you for blessings that you will receive in the future.

You make your way easily down the other side of the mountain, enjoying the flora and fauna you see along the way. At the end of the path, your Higher Self is waiting. He or she presents you with a small gift box. Inside is a valuable message regarding your future.

Diving for Dollars

Picture yourself sitting by a beatiful swimming pool. Imagine the largest swimming pool that you can, as water represents psychic energy. Who is sitting with you? How are they dressed? Are they smiling or frowning? If you don't like their energy, bid them farewell. Replace their image with that of well-dressed, friendly companions.

Imagine that the pool is surrounded by a garden full of beautiful blooming plants of all kinds. Imagine yourself circling the outside of the pool in a clockwise direction, admiring each flower in turn. Make sure you take the time to smell each one.

Picture yourself climbing up to the diving board and looking down into the pool. When you look down, you see that it is not full of water but cash. It is filled to the brim with bills of all denominations—$5, $100 and $1000 bills. You can elaborate on this visualization to include foreign currency, checks or bank drafts.

Take a deep breath and dive into the pool of money. As you dive in notice how the money feels against your skin. Swim. Splash about. Clean your skin with the money. Picture yourself floating on a buoyant bed of cash.

Chapter Five

Candle Burning Rituals

It is better to light a single flame than to curse the darkness. Ritual candle burning falls into several categories: color vibration, moon phase, petition to the saints, petition to the angels, and petition to the deities and spirits. Candle burning is practiced in almost every culture and religion: Roma (gypsy culture), Catholicism, Santeria, Paganism, Celtic traditions and Egyptian schools of magic. Candle burning is also a part of Angel Magic and many New Age practices.

There are two schools of thought as to how candle burning works best. Occult-oriented religions see candle burning as a way to build energy towards an intention. Other religions use the light of the candle as a way of sending a problem, usually through the smoke, up to the care of a Higher Power. Usually the request is scratched into the candle or placed on a piece of parchment paper beneath the candle for a number of days.

Candle Burning 101

One of the questions I am asked most frequently is "what color of candle should I burn for what purpose?" Since there is no book out there called Candle Burning for Dummies, here is a crash course in candles and their corresponding magical purposes. As a practicing ceromancer, the first thing you must learn is how to pray your heart out and laugh maniacally. As far as I'm concerned, no spell is complete without fervent wishing and praying followed by a maniacal laugh to seal the spell.

The second thing you must do is familiarize yourself with the phases of the moon. It is best to practice most magic between the New Moon and the Full Moon period when the Moon is waxing. The Moon waxes during the fourteen-day period when it goes from New to the Full Moon. During this period, cosmic or astral energy is building and this is the best time for attracting a lover, more money, more gerbils or whatever. The period between the Full Moon and the next New Moon is best for banishing spells and getting rid of negativity, stalkers and the like. Go to www.artcharts.com for more information.

Red candles burnt during the waxing moon period are used to attract more drama and war-like energy into your life. In business you would burn a red candle to increase ambition and drive.

Orange candles bring love, joy, happiness, feasting and luck with children and pets. These candles draw business to those in the hospitality or entertainment industry.

Green candles increase cash flow and bring steady work. They represent abundance and opportunity. Combined with a black candle during the waning moon, green candles can help remove financial obstacles.

Yellow candles are for both spiritual and material riches and help align your will with your heart. Yellow is the color to burn if you are confused about your career or professional matters. Yellow candles can also help you find the discipline to save for that new car.

Pink candles help you manifest the higher qualities of love: patience, faith and compassion. Pink can help you choose the right artistic career.

Brown candles help ground your energies to the earth

and make you feel connected to reality. Burning a brown candle can make you feel more confident about business matters.

Blue candles help you focus and find solutions to your problems. Blue is associated with peace and mercy, so it is a good candle to burn if you feel oppressed by creditors.

Purple candles can be decadent or holy, depending your intention, when burning. Purple is the color of the eccentric, the bon vivant, the wise and the royal. Purple is the candle to burn if you need to increase sales or receive good reviews and awards.

Violet is the color of the Higher Self, and is a good candle to burn when you need to connect to yours. Violet enhances intuitive abilities and is a good choice when you feel you need to let go of someone or something. Stare at the flame and throw all your worries, burdens and concerns into the violet fire.

I rarely burn black candles and I don't know why. **Black** candles are grounding and often associated with negative rituals and energies; on the other hand, they are also used for protection, and are a good choice if you feel sabotaged. As the black candle burns, picture all the negative energy melting away.

White candles are all-purpose. When in doubt, use a white candle. A white candle burnt with another color clears the energies, allowing the color to resonate through space. Used alone, white candles represent peace, purity and the connection to angels and whoever you perceive God to be.

Remember that when you burn a candle, it is your intent that matters the most. This kind of ritual depends on synchronicity, so make sure that when you make your wish, you picture or act out the scenario in your mind as vividly as you can. And don't forget to laugh maniacally when you're finished. The cosmos likes a person with a sense of humor.

Classic Candle Burning for Prosperity

There are many commercial candles on the market that are intended to bring prosperity.

The most common kind of candle on the shelves is the Seven-Day Candle which is wax encased in a tall glass pillar. The intention of these candles is expressed in illustrations on the glass. The candles usually have labels such as Money Drawing Power or Money Magnet and are often subtly scented with a money-drawing oil, such as patchouli or jasmine.

One of the most traditional commercial candles used for money-drawing purposes is the bayberry candle. Usually this candle will sport the old saying "A bayberry candle burned to the socket brings prosperity to the family and money in the pocket." You can also buy a regular bayberry candle and burn it for the same purpose.

Occult shops carry molded candles, such as the Black Cat and the Lucky Hand. Both are burned for luck at gaming and gambling. Some candles feature keys and clover leaves on a burning cross. These are called the Master Key Crucifix Candles. The green version of this candle is used to draw money and the orange version to encourage change.

Another candle on the market is the Seven-Knob Wishing Candle, which looks like a stack of flattened spheres. The idea is to place a petition or request underneath this candle and burn down one sphere a day for seven days.

Many New Age stores also sell candles that offer the

intents of different magical purposes. When unsure as to what kind of candle to burn for prosperity, burn a beeswax candle, since honeybee wax represents prosperity.

Below is a compendium of candle burning rituals from many cultures that are used to draw prosperity.

The Simplest Money-Drawing Ritual: Anoint any green candle with olive oil. Light the candle and say a general prayer requesting the money you need from the universe.

Simple Money Wish Ritual: At five o'clock or eight o'clock on the night of the New Moon, write your wish on a clean piece of paper. Light a white candle and turn off all the lights. Think about the fulfillment of your wish for several minutes, then burn the paper in the flame of the candle. Repeat this ritual at the same time for twelve consecutive nights.

"Cash In a Hurry" Spiritual Prescription: This is a low-budget spell for quick cash that I often prescribe for my clients. You will need: one green or gold candle, cinnamon, honey, orange oil, orange water or juice and eight copper pennies.

First, take a blank check. In any color ink except red (green or gold is best), write the check out to yourself in the amount that you need to immediately get out of trouble plus a little extra for fun. Decorate the check with dollar signs and hearts - make it yours! Scratch your initials into the side of the candle, and anoint it lightly with a bit of honey. Dab orange essence on it, stroking outwards towards the end from the middle of the candle. The orange essence represents your willingness to receive money as well as joy. After this, lightly sprinkle cinnamon or sugar cinnamon on the candle to ensure the money's swift arrival.

Place the check beneath the candle. Arrange the eight copper pennies in a circle around it. Eight is the number of prosperity.

Light the candle and say:

"By the power of three times three, I ask that (state amount) be sent to me. I ask that all the money I need be sent with speed. I ask that this be done in this hour in full power according to the will of God, helping all and harming none. Amen."

Let the candle burn all the way down (using a small candle is a good idea so you burn it in one night or in a couple of hours). Remember to never leave a candle burning unattended.

As the candle burns, picture money coming to you and imagine yourself surrendering your financial problems to a Higher Power (God or the Archangel Chamuel). Swear to yourself that you are not going to worry. After the candle is burnt down take the eight pennies to a playground and place them where a child can find them—at the bottom of a slide, in a sandbox, or under a swing. This is your way of giving surprise back to the Universe. Take the check, put it in an envelope and hide it in a safe place. When I seal the envelope, I make sure I am wearing lipstick and kiss it before I close it. Make this wish yours.

Quick Money Ritual to Pay A Bill: Anoint the candle with cinnamon oil. Take the bill or write the amount that is owed on a piece of paper. You will need a green candle that can burn for seven days. Place the paper under the candle. Hold your hands over it and say,

"This candle burns to light the way,
To help me prosper and help me pay
The bill(s) that were due yesterday.
I ask this money come with all speed
And that money be supplied to others in need.
Amen."

Light the candle and burn patchouli incense. Meditate for five minutes as the candle burns. Visualize yourself writing the check or depositing the money you need to pay the bill. Burn the candle every day at eight in the morning or eight in the evening for eight minutes. On the eighth day, put the paper with your request on it in the flame and let the candle burn out completely.

As Above, So Below Ritual

Scratch the amount of money that you need on the side of a green, gold or yellow candle and place it on a small pocket mirror. Light the candle and state the amount of money you need. Then say "As Above, So Below." The idea is that the candle reflected in the mirror stretches the reach of this request into the unconscious realms and mirrors its manifestation into reality.

To Obtain $500

Light a green candle and rub your hands in the smoke of the flame. Ask the Universe for the sum of $500. Apparently this does not work for any other amount, but it works fast.

Urgent Money Prescription: You will need: a tall pillar candle in gold, silver, green or white, several votive candles (preferably green or gold), and a plate that you eat off frequently.

This ritual is best performed daily on a New Moon or a Full Moon. It works best fifteen minutes before midnight.

Use one votive candle to represent each $100 or $1000 that you need. Place the votive candles in a circle with the tall pillar candle in the middle. The pillar candle represents you and the votive candles represent the amount of money that you want to receive.

Light the pillar candle first (you may personalize the candle by scratching your initials into the wax first).

Pick up one of the votive candles and light it from the main candle flame that represents you. As you do so, state out loud that the votive you are lighting represents the $100 or $1000 you need. Place it on the plate to begin a circle of "money" candles.

Light each votive, and say the same words for each until the circle is complete.

Say a prayer explaining why the money is necessary. Thank the powers above for the total amount of money you have requested. Let the candles burn out.

Chocolate Coins Candle Ritual: Surround a green or gold candle with coins wrapped in colored foil. The number of coins that you use for this spell depends on what you need. Each coin represents a desire, or an amount of money that you need to pay a bill. Light the candle and state your request. As the candle burns down, unwrap the chocolate foil and eat the chocolate while focusing on each desire.

Spiritual Prescription for Wealth: When the moon is New or Full in the signs of Scorpio or Leo, light one black, one silver, one gold and one red candle. Burning this combination of colors is good for manifesting larger and more luxurious material objects.

To Remove Prosperity Blocks: Light one green candle and one black candle during the waning phase of the moon cycle. Visualize the financial problems that you would like to see disappear. If you feel that a spiritual malaise accentuates your problem, you may add a white candle. If someone is gossiping or maligning your professional reputation, then add a red candle to the equation.

For Prosperity and Happy Surprises: Light one pink, one yellow, one gold and one silver candle to attract unexpected good fortune into your life. This combination of colors attracts the assistance of good spirits and fairies.

Solstice Money-Drawing Ritual: Perform this spell one minute past midnight on the evening of each solstice. The solstices are April 30th(May 1st), July 31st (August 1st), October 31st (November 1st) and January 31st (February 1st).

You will need one gold candle, six green candles, nine white candles, pine oil and salt.

Anoint all candles with pine oil and then arrange them as follows: the gold candle sits in the center, the green candles circle the gold candle, and the white candles circle the green ones.

At one minute past midnight on the appointed day, sprinkle salt around the outermost perimeter of the candles. Light the gold candle first, then the green and then the white, making sure you are moving in a clockwise direction. Sit quietly for a few minutes and visualize the solutions to your financial problems. Then take a candle snuffer and gently put out the candles in the reverse order that you lit them.

Chapter Six

Angels and Saints of Prosperity
Angels

An angel can be your best friend. Angels have been known to respond to prayers that contain one word: "HELP!!!"

Angels should be treated like guests invited into your heart. Like most guests, they tend to leave or ignore an environment that is filled with hostility. So before you call on an angel, meditate, picture your heart as a soft place, and light a candle that is attractive to that particular heavenly being.

Before calling on an angel for financial help, prepare your heart to receive its presence. Speak the angel's name out loud. Talk to the angel as you would to a treasured friend, not as a withholding parent who won't grant your wish. Don't demand immediate gratification and don't be so rude as to interrupt if you start to hear a message. If you are silent and respectful, fervent and loving, an angel will always give you the answer you need to solve your problem.

Make your request specific, and visualize what you would like if you can, but don't be attached to the outcome. Angels are agents of the Lord and like God, they work in mysterious ways.

Here is a list of the Seven Archangels, their functions and corresponding light rays:

Archangel Michael is the Angel of Protection and corresponds to the color blue. You can ask him for protection from financial trouble as well as attacks on your reputation. Pray to the Archangel Michael if you are suffering from oppression from the tax department or creditors, or if you feel optionless. He is the Angel that can protect you as you proceed down a difficult but necessary path, such as declaring bankruptcy.

Archangel Jophiel is the Angel of Illumination and corresponds to the color yellow. Pray to the Archangel Jophiel if you are at a crossroads when it comes to making important decisions regarding finances and career.

Archangel Chamuel is the Angel of Love and corresponds to the color pink. Pray to this angel if you need to find a new job. Chamuel's pink rays can also help dissolve feelings of self-condemnation and low self-esteem. Pray to the Archangel Chamuel when you are concerned about how to keep a roof over your head and food on the table. It is Chamuel that supplies us with our daily bread and ensures that we have the tools and transportation that we need to do our daily work.

Archangel Gabriel is the Angel of Guidance and corresponds to the color white. This angel can help you organize and streamline your life, as well as provide you with advice regarding your education and career. He is also the angel to pray to if you need a new item for your home. Gabriel is the archangel to pray to if you need of clarity about which career path to take. He can also help remove prosperity blocks from your past that may be lowering your ability to attract prosperity. Materially, Gabriel can also help manifest the right clothes for a job interview or necessary equipment such as a computer.

Archangel Raphael is the Angel of Healing and corresponds to the color green. Raphael is responsible for the healing of body, mind, soul and spirit and can help put your daily bread on the table. Pray to

Raphael when you are in need of clothing, food or shelter. Pray to Raphael if you are in debt or in a hopeless financial situation. Raphael can also help individuals travel through difficult yet necessary paths such as a change of career.

Archangel Uriel is the Angel of Peace and corresponds to the colors purple and gold. Uriel resolves all problems in personal, social and professional relationships and helps to create harmony in your life. Appeal to Uriel if you need help negotiating a contract or if you are having trouble dealing with creditors. He can also help expedite the passage of cash to those who have been waiting a long time for money.

Archangel Zadkiel is the Angel of Joy and corresponds to the color violet. This is the angel to pray to if you need work as an actor, writer or performer. Pray to Zadkiel when you feel dissatisfied with your financial situation and have forgotten how to be thankful for all of the blessings that you DO have.

Saints

Petitioning the Saints for special favors is a tradition in both Catholic and Santeria religions.

When you ask the Catholic Saints for help, it is common to write your request on a piece of paper and place it beneath the appropriately colored candle. If there is a totem animal, emblem or object that you associate with you can place that item on the saint's altar as well. If you can find a picture of the Saint in a religious store and place it on the altar, that is even better.

Saint Cecilia: Burn a green candle on a Wednesday for success in a career in the arts, particularly if you are a musician, poet or singer. Her emblem is an organ.

Saint Frances Xavier Cabrini: Burn a white candle on a Sunday to help with matters of immigration or for matters pertaining to health, education or insurance.

Saint Philomena: Burn a pink or green candle on a Saturday to help with desperate situations such as problems with children, unhappiness in the home, and providing food for the poor. Philomena is a favorite saint of single mothers. Her symbol is an anchor.

Saint Anthony of Padua: Burn a candle on a Tuesday for special requests or a green candle for financial help. His emblem is the lily.

Saint Benedict: Burn a white candle on a Saturday to ask for increased prosperity and faith. His emblem is a raven or a broken cup.

Saint Florian: Burn a red or orange candle on a Sunday to protect the home. Pray to Saint Florian for help with any kind of emergency that has to do with the home such as a flood, fire, or infestation. His emblem is a burning torch under the foot.

Saint James the Greater: Light a red candle on a Tuesday to clear obstacles from your path, conquer enemies and make justice prevail. His emblem is a cockle shell.

Saint John the Baptist: Light a green candle on a Tuesday to petition him for good luck, fertility, prosperity and protection from enemies.

Saint Joseph: Light a yellow candle on a Sunday for help with selling a home or finding a job. His emblem is a lily.

Saint Lawrence: Light a red candle on a Wednesday to ask for a happy home and family, financial assistance and spiritual strength.

Saint Jude: Light green, white and red candles on a

Sunday to petition for a miracle in cases of extreme poverty.

Saint Martin Caballero: Light a red or white candle on a Tuesday to draw customers to your business.

Saint Patrick: Light a white candle on a Sunday for prosperity, luck, spiritual wisdom and guidance. His emblem is a shamrock and a snake.

Saint Peter: Light a red and a white candle to petition him to remove obstacles and increase business success and good fortune. His emblem is two crossed keys.

Chapter Seven

Gods and Goddesses of Prosperity

Thousands of Gods and Goddesses from all cultures govern the four pillars of prosperity: health, freedom, happiness and love. Below is a compendium of the most traditional deities in each culture plus a short description of their purpose. If a God or Goddess appeals to you, obtain a picture of that deity and ask him or her for help through prayer and candle burning.

Indian Gods and Goddesses

Brahma: God of the Trinity. Pray to him for health, wealth and happiness and spiritual oneness with God.

Durga: Also known as Shakti (Life Energy) and Parvati (Family Unity). Pray to her for general abundance and matters to do with family, child-rearing and the home.

Ganesha: God who Removes Obstacles, God of Knowledge. Pray to him for opportunity and direction in life.

Gauri: Goddess of Purity and Austerity. Pray to her when you feel guilty about overspending money.

Krishna: God of Power and Bravery. Pray to him when faced with a tough financial or career decision.

Lakshmi: Goddess of Prosperity, Purity, Chastity and Generosity. An excellent Goddess to ask for gifts, cash and opportunities of all kinds.

Sarasvati: Goddess of Speech, Wisdom and Learning. Pray to her for assistance with job interviews or in situations where you need confidence.

Shiva: God of Giving and Happiness, Creator. Pray to him for general prosperity.

Vishnu: God of Courage, Knowledge and Power. Also known as Hari the Remover. Pray to him when uncertain about your path or when making a difficult financial decision.

Japanese Gods and Goddesses
Uzume: Shinto Goddess of joy, happiness and good health. Pray to her for general abundance.

Toyo-Uke-Bime: Goddess of earth, agriculture and food. Pray to her for shelter, work and to always be blessed with food on the table.

Schichi Fukujin: A laughing God with a big round belly that represents laughter, happiness, and the wisdom of contentment. Pray to him to relish every living moment.

Chinese Gods and Goddesses
Ch'eng-Huang: God of Moats and Walls. Pray to him for protection against creditors.

Kwan Yin: Goddess of Mercy and Compassion. Pray to her for daily essentials and for protection in financially unstable situations.

Ti-Tsang Wang: God of Mercy. Pray to him when stuck in a financial corner.

T'shai-shen: God of Wealth. Pray to him when you need a bill paid.

Tsao Wang: God of the Hearth and Family. Pray to him to assure health, wealth, happiness and well-fed tummies.

African Gods and Goddesses
Elegua: Also known as Esu. Pray to him to open the door to new financial and career opportunities.

Leza (Rhodesia): Creator who is Compassionate and

Merciful. Pray to him for financial assistance.

Oshun: Goddess of Love and Money. Pray to her for health, wealth and love.

Egyptian Gods and Goddesses

Amun: King of the Gods. Pray to him for general prosperity.

Atum: First God, God of Perfection. Pray to him for balance in your life.

Horus: God of the Sky, Ruler of Egypt. Pray to for the proper circulation of money in your life and for ever-renewing cycles of prosperity.

Isis: Goddess of Protection and Magic. Pray to her for financial miracles.

Ma'at: Goddess of Truth, Justice and Harmony. Pray to her when things seem out of balance or during a run of bad luck.

Ra: Sun God. Pray to him for delightful surprises, wealth and abundance.

Seshat: Goddess of Writing and Measurement. Pray to her when applying for a job in writing, banking, accounting, physics or architecture.

Thoth: God of Writing and Knowledge. Pray to when applying for jobs in creative fields.

Sumerian Gods and Goddesses

An: God of the Heavens. Pray to him for prosperity.

Enki: Lord of Water and Wisdom. Pray to him for positive thinking and miraculous manifestations from the unconscious.

Inanna: Goddess of Love and War. Pray to her for general abundance and prosperity.

Greek and Roman Gods and Goddesses

Apollo (Greek); **Mercury** (Roman): Gods of Civilization and the Arts. Pray to them for success with jobs related to the humanities.

Artemis (Greek); **Diana** (Roman): Goddesses of Childbirth and Hunting. Pray to them for discipline, clarity of thought and the ability to achieve deadlines and goals.

Athena (Greek); **Minerva** (Roman): Goddesses of War, Wisdom and the Arts. Pray to them for self-confidence when applying for a job.

Dionysius (Greek); **Bacchus** (Roman): Gods of Wine. Pray to then to achieve luxuries in life.

Hecate (Greek): Goddess of the Underworld, Witchcraft and Black Magic. Pray to her for swift changes, self-confidence and miracles.

Hera (Greek): Goddess of Marriage, Family and the Home. Pray to her for general abundance.

Hermes (Greek); **Mercury** (Roman): Gods of Merchants. Pray to them for better business, before making a speech or proposal or when applying for a job as a politician or writer.

Hestia (Greek): Goddess of Hearth, Fire and Family Life. Pray to her for abundance and financial security.

Zeus (Greek); **Jupiter** (*Roman*): Kings of the Greek Pantheon of Gods. Pray to them for miracles and special favors.

Persephone (Greek): Goddess of Fertility and Nature. Pray to her for faith in ever-renewing cycles and for the wisdom to spend wisely.

Celtic Gods and Goddesses

Cernunnos: The 'Horned God,' God of Nature, Animals,

Fertility and the Underworld. Pray to him for success in business.

Coventina: Goddess of Rivers, Abundance, Inspiration and Prophecy. Pray to her for financial assistance.

Eostre: Goddess of Spring, Rebirth, Fertility and New Beginnings. Pray to her when looking for a new job.

Epona: Horse Goddess, Goddess of Prosperity, Healing and Sustenance. Pray to her for assistance with job hunting and money management.

Lugh: Sun God, God of War, Mastery, Magic and Good Harvests. Pray to him for wise financial decisions or when investing in stocks.

Scottish, Irish and Welsh Gods and Goddesses

Oghma (Scottish, Irish): God of Communication and Writing, and God of Poets. Pray to him before a job interview or in a situation that involves self-promotion, writing talent and eloquence of speech.

Rhiannon (Welsh): Goddess of Birds, Horses, Enchantments, Fertility and the Underworld. Pray to her for the persistence of good fortune.

Norse Gods and Goddesses

Freya: Goddess of Love, Beauty, War, Magic and Wisdom. Pray to her for protection of your home and family.

Freyr: God of Fertility and Success. Pray to him for assistance with your finances and career.

Frigga: Goddess Mother of All, Protector of Children. Pray to her for a prosperous life and a peaceful home.

Chapter Eight

Charms and Talismans for Prosperity

Many of you already own several lucky charms or talismans. But you may not be aware of the objects' symbolism. Below is a list of some of the more popular good luck symbols that can be purchased in the form of jewelry, paintings or statues.

The Clover: The three-leafed clover is a symbol of health and vitality. For the Celts, it symbolizes The Holy Trinity. A four-leafed clover symbolizes good fortune. A five-leafed clover symbolizes a happy marriage.

The Pentagram: This five-sided star is also known as the Druid's Foot. As a talisman, it serves to fulfill wishes, invoke spiritual powers and activate inner ones. It also serves as a protective amulet against the "evil eye."

The Star of David: This six-pointed star is also known as the Seal of Solomon and the Hexagram. It consists of two interlocking triangles and is used as a talisman to attain harmony.

Thor's Hammer: This talisman looks like a small axe or a blunt-edged cross. Carrying this symbol helps to achieve social success and protects against making the wrong career move. It also helps prevent losses on the stock market!

The Medicine Wheel: For about 5,000 years, almost all Native American tribes have designed some form of medicine wheel. The design varies, but medicine wheels are Mandalas whose imagery is based on the number four, which represents the four pillars of prosperity. Medicine Wheels help develop personal power and equilibrium, attain wisdom and understand the ups and downs of life.

Roman Coins: Antique Roman coins bring prosperity and good fortune to those who wear them as jewelry.

Roots and animal parts are also thought to inspire good fortune, especially if carried on one's person:

Alligator's Tooth, Alligator's Foot, or Bat Hearts: Carried by gamblers in the American South for good luck.

Nutmeg: A nutmeg husk is hollowed out, filled with silver and sealed with wax as a good luck charm for gamblers.

Buckeye: This seed is considered a lucky hoodoo charm for gamblers.

American Mercury Dime: This American currency, which sports a winged image of the god Mercury on one side, brings about financial windfalls.

Lodestone: These naturally magnetic stones are often dressed with magnetic sand and carried in the pocket to "attract" money.

John the Conquerer Root: This type of root resembles a hand and is carried for luck.

Certain animals and statues are also thought to bring luck:

The Lucky Millionaire Cat (Chinese): This ceramic cat, with its right hand raised, brings good fortune to a business.

Goldfish (Chinese): Images or statues of goldfish are thought to bring prosperity. A poster boasting eight goldfish and one black goldfish brings protection as well as prosperity to a business.

Tortoise (Chinese): This charm is used to hold onto money, invest it wisely and create wealth.

Lucky Money Frog (Chinese): This small ceramic statue of a frog holds a coin in its mouth. Placed near the front door of a home or place of business, the frog draws prosperity.

Whale (Northwest American Indian): The Whale brings prosperity, wisdom and longevity.

Otter (Prairie Indian): The otter represents joy, protection of family and financial success.

Falcon (Prairie Indian): The falcon brings insight, wisdom and the ability to connect with the Higher Self.

Rabbit (Prairie Indian): The rabbit symbolizes fertility, abundance and prosperity.

Elk (Prairie Indian): The elk helps to find the right occupation and to enjoy working.

Turtle (Prairie Indian): The turtle is a symbol of financial security and peace.

Butterfly (American Indian): The butterfly represents love, grace, abundance, inspiration, passion and blessings.

Wolf (American Indian): The wolf is a symbol of leadership qualities.

Hippopotamus (East Indian): This animal represents luck, love, money and prosperity.

Elephant (East Indian, African): This enormous animal represents prosperity and wisdom.

Runes, which are stones used for fortune-telling, can also be worn to attract prosperity. The symbols on Runes usually represent animals. The best ones to wear for prosperity are; UROZ (power; ox), FEHU (possession; livestock), KENAZ (opportunity; the torch), WUNJO (happiness; an X) or JERA (harvest; interlocking Vs).

Some individuals might also want to sport charms bearing the traditionally lucky numbers such as one (for primacy and unity); three (to represent the Holy Trinity and the Unity of the three planes of consciousness); four (for universal balance of all components in a human life); five (which in Tibetan traditions is linked with the Divine Imagination); six (for gambling luck as it represents the highest number on a dice); seven (an old superstition links this with luck); eight(the Chinese number for prosperity); and nine (the number of renewal, rebirth and karma).

Chapter Nine

Prosperity Is In the Earth: Plants, Herbs and Roots

Plants, herbs and roots have been used for centuries to draw money to a person or bring prosperity to a home.

There are several ways to use a plant in this manner:

You can easily carry a tiny piece of herb in a plastic bag in your pocket or put a pinch of herb in a locket.

You can sew a sachet or pouch and fill it with an herb. You can buy ready-made sachets or pouches for this purpose, but you can also sew a small one using an appropriately colored material. Green and yellow are popular colors associated with prosperity and money. Tuck the sachet under your bed, wear it on a string around your neck, or put it in your purse or wallet. Some people simply fill a pot-pourri jar with the appropriate herb and place the jar in a prominent place in the house.

The simplest Wiccan "Earth, Water, Air, Fire" Ritual is to boil the herb in a pot of water on the stove. The herb represents the earth, the water is in the pot, the air is the steam and the fire element is the stove. Stir the herb occasionally while thinking of your magical intention. Then strain the plant material from the liquid and sprinkle the remaining infusion around or outside the home.

You can use herbs as incense. Since some plants are hypnotics, however, I don't recommend you use plants as incense unless you are certain that the herb is not toxic once set alight. Traditionally though, herbs are set alight on charcoal burners and the smoke is allowed to waft through the house.

Here are some of the more popular herbs used to

draw prosperity and money. Most are available in your garden or from occult shops and apothecaries.

Alfalfa: This is known traditionally as the "good luck" herb. Tuck a sprig of this in your purse or in a locket. When combined with other money-drawing herbs in a sachet, alfalfa reinforces the other substance's powers.

Allspice: This herb can be carried on your person, or burned as incense or sprinkled in four corners of the room. Allspice attracts business luck or success.

Bayberry: Bayberry can be bought commercially as a candle or as incense.

Chamomile: Some gamblers wash their hands in chamomile tea for good luck. Drinking chamomile tea brings luck and prosperity.

Citronella: The leaves are good for attracting business and also smell lovely in a pot-pourri.

Cloves: Cloves can be burned on charcoal, tucked in a sachet or put in your purse to draw money. An ancient ritual is to cover an orange with cloves and hang it on a ribbon in the kitchen to keep the cupboards from ever becoming bare.

Five-Finger Grass (also known as **Cinquefoil**): This lemony grass can be burned, hid in a potpourri or carried on your person. It is the standard ingredient in most money-drawing incenses.

Grains of Paradise: These little round seeds can be carried in the purse or wallet or tucked in a sachet under a pillow to bring luck and guidance in career or money matters.

Honeysuckle: The fresh and dried flowers of this plant are used to attract luck in business. When used with other herbs, honeysuckle quickens prosperity.

Irish Moss: This is a seaweed that can be bought in Caribbean stores. Traditionally used to make a sweet drink, Irish Moss is also carried in sachets to bring money to the bearer.

Juniper Berries: Associated with Jupiter, the berries of the juniper tree are attract luck, good fortune and business success.

Patchouli: Added to prosperity herb mixes, patchouli reinforces the manifestation power of wishes. It is good for a growing business.

Strawberry Leaves: Carried in the pocket, strawberry leaves are used to draw fortunate circumstances into your life.

Squill Root: Although difficult to find,, this root is one of the most powerful plants used to draw money to the bearer.

Tonka Beans: Tonkas are large dried beans that protect against poverty and are considered lucky. Place a bean in your purse, near your computer or under your phone—anywhere you need luck in business.

Magic In Your Spice Rack

Variety is the spice of life, but historically spices are the stuff of magic! A magic spell, after all is simply a recipe and many spells traditionally involve using plants or herbs. Magic doesn't have to be complicated to work. In fact, the simplest spells sometimes work best of all, because they most resemble an innocent wish and the doer is not attached to the outcome. Check out the magical uses of some of these common spices, which are found in almost everybody's spice rack at home.

Basil: Said to be ruled by Mars, basil has a protective and cleansing influence. If you have had contact with

someone you dislike and whose negative energy
seems to be hanging around, a bit of basil steeped in
warm water and drunk like a tea or mixed with
tobacco and burned on the tip of a cigarette will
drive the obnoxious influence away. Basil sprinkled
near the front door will bring you money.

Bay Leaf: Aside from seasoning stew, the bay leaf can
also be used for granting wishes. Write your wish on
a piece of paper, place three bay leaves inside and
fold it into thirds. Fold the paper into thirds again.
Once your wish has been granted, the paper and bay
leaves should be burned as a thank you. Bathing in
bay leaves (add nine of them to a bath) will bring you
fame and glory.

Cinnamon: Cinnamon is one of the most useful spices in
practical magic and is used to purify, bless and protect things and improve communication. Sprinkling
a little cinnamon on your toast or your café latte in
the morning may help to improve business.
Cinnamon is ruled by Mercury, therefore sucking on
a cinnamon-flavored candy before you make a presentation or give a speech can help you be more eloquent.

Ginger: Ginger is used to speed things up. Next time
you wash your floor, add a little ginger and cinnamon to the water in the pail to make your own "Fast
Luck in a Hurry" floor wash. A little ginger sprinkled
under the phone may cause that important call to
come faster, but don't use too much ... it can also
cause a heated argument.

Mint: If you need to sparkle in a crowd, charm, woo, or
sell something, try nibbling on a little mint or drinking mint tea before you do your presentation.
Sucking on a spearmint-flavored Tic-Tac will do the

trick as well.

Parsley: Need some cold hard cash? Make a tea out of dried parsley by adding a teaspoon of the dried herb to a cup of boiled water. Add it to your bath or put it in an atomizer. Sprinkle or spray the parsley water in a clockwise direction in your house to raise your money-drawing vibration.

Sage: Sage is an herb of wisdom. A tea made from a teaspoon of sage and a cup of boiling water can be added to the bathtub or sprinkled throughout the house to help destroy illusions and raise mental clarity. You can also buy sage commercially in tea bags, and drink it to help improve your memory while studying for tests.

Salt: Salt has been used for ages to purify spaces and prevent negative energies from entering your home. Try sprinkling a little in all four corners of the house for protection. Taking a bath in salt will to purify your aura.

Flowers and Houseplants

When you find yourself stuck in a chronic pattern, it usually means that your personality has somehow temporarily disconnected from your Higher Self. The traditional quick fix for reconnecting to your Higher Self is to spend some time in nature. Half an hour spent by a stream or pond can do more for your body and soul than any self-help book, years of psychotherapy, or a prescription for Prozac. Once you return home, however, you might find yourself drawn down again spiritually and emotionally by the dull and oppressive vibes hanging around your environment. The spiritual remedy for this problem is to bring a bit of nature inside to raise the vibrations in your home. Plants have a natural connection to the higher realms that you can access just by having them in your energy field.

Whenever I feel stuck in a rut, I buy myself a new houseplant. I usually do this when I feel surrounded by stale energy, or if I'm feeling bored, frustrated or discouraged. This stale energy often manifests itself on the physical plane—the phone never rings, loved ones and pets seem irritable, and bills arrive long before the money is there to pay them.

Different houseplants have specific influences and powers. For instance, if you feel in need of protection, try placing an aloe vera, cactus, fern, ivy or Venus Flytrap near your entrances and exits. Pick something low maintenance, like a palm tree or an ivy plant, which is also thought to attract prosperity.

However, nothing is better than roses to give you a lift and raise the vibrations in your home. Roses are traditionally associated with such compassionate female deities as The Virgin Mary, Quan Yin and Aphrodite. I like to buy a rose (or bouquet) and recite the following poem by Elizabeth Clare Prophet: "As a rose unfolding fair, Wafts her fragrance on the air, I pour forth to God devotion, One now with the cosmic ocean." I visualize my entire home being bathed in pink, violet or white light and the next thing I know, the phone is ringing off the hook, I have been paid, and Prince Charming is standing at the door.

Gemstones

The New Age should also be called The Stone Age, because along with aromatherapy, healing with the vibrations and frequencies emitted by gemstones is at the crux of the movement. Below is a list of seven popular gemstones that draw prosperity with the divine energies of the Seven Archangels. If you don't own any jewelry you can buy inexpensive, unpolished gems in stores or on the Internet. Once you have the stone, it is best to wear it, which is why so many gems are set in necklaces, bracelets and rings. Some people like to purify an unpolished stone after purchasing it by dropping it in a glass of salt and leaving it overnight. In the case of used jewelry, you might want to do this to cleanse it of the energies of the previous owner.

Not everyone can afford the classic gems used to draw prosperity such as rubies, sapphires and diamonds, but there are many semi-precious stones that can raise vibration to attract prosperity.

Agate: Agate increases perceptions and awakens hidden talents.

Amber: Amber absorbs negative energy and transforms it into positive energy, calms nerves and heals.

Carnelian: This gem dispels laziness, rage, jealousy, envy and fear. It is also good for encouraging creativity.

Citrine: This money-drawing stone also cheers and clears the aura.

Hematite: Hematite improves the intellect, gives protection, and transforms negative energy to positive energy.

Jade: Jade is for luck.

Lapis Lazuli: This blue gem is used for esoteric mysteries, channeling, and awareness.

Moonstone: Moonstone represents the new

Peridot: Peridot attracts friends, cleanses the heart, and encourages happiness.

Quartz (smoky): This stone dissolves negative energies

and resentment; it also enhances self-esteem and attracts business.

Sandstone: Sandstone stimulates creativity, helps build solidarity, and improves your social life.

Topaz: Topaz fosters true love, success, joy, attraction, manifestation, and healing.

Tourmaline: This gem encourages harmony, unconditional love, and intuition.

Turquoise: Turquoise improves communication, intuition, creativity, protection, and wisdom

Zircon: This stone inspires strength and virtue, and helps integrate body and mind.

Chapter Ten

Simple Rituals and Spells
Prosperity Practices

Sometimes, the most absurd and smallest practice works better than a ritual that requires a dramatic production. The following practices are more along the lines of superstition, but I have tried them and they have worked at one time or another.

Every time you see a coin on the floor, stomp on it and say "Money on the floor, money on the door!" Then pick it up and put it in your wallet.

Always keep a bowl of small change, (foreign or old coins are best) in a bowl by your front door. Antique or old keys attract money as well.

Buy a jade plant, a blue-green succulent with big fleshy leaves. Put it by the front door or in the northeast corner of your home or office. Keep the leaves clean and free from dust.

Write a check to yourself for the total amount of money you need and the date you need it by. Use a gold pen and make the check look as official as possible. Anoint the check with Money Drawing Oil, which can be bought commercially, or use bergamot, vetivert, cinnamon or orange oil. Fold the check eight times and put it in a dark place.

Make a money tree, preferably at Christmas (though you can do it at any time of the year). Find an old branch and attach money to it with clothespins. The idea is that whatever you attach is worth ten times as much. For instance, if you attach a $5 bill, it actually represents $50. Don't have any money? You can use monopoly money or even attach green slips of paper with the denominations written on them. I know it sounds nuts, but I have experienced surprising results with this practice.

Keep little pots of rosemary, sage, parsley, thyme and basil at your front door or on your windowsill. These herbs are thought to draw money to you as long as they are kept healthy.

Make a God Box. Find a box you like. Any size will do. Decorate it with images that will represent how serene you will feel once you are out of debt. Make a little opening in the top. If you find yourself in need, write your request on a piece of paper and drop it in the box. I did this one year and at the end of the year as I looked over my requests I was amazed at how many of my wishes had been taken care of...about 90%. The reason this practice works is that once you spell your wish out, you detach yourself from the anxiety of the matter and its outcome because you have given your problem to a Higher Power to take care of.

Magical Baths

Creating a Magical Bath is as simple as going to your local drug or beauty supply store and buying a product that is appropriately scented with herbs or essential oils. The important thing about a Magical Bath, no matter how humble or expensive the ingredients are, is to meditate on your intention while you are in the tub.

You can get fancier by making an infusion from flowers, herbs or other elements. Brewing the herbs as you would brew a cup of herbal tea and then pouring the strained water into your bath water is the easiest way to make an infusion. You can also put the ingredients in a cheesecloth bag and let hot water run through it. You can even buy tea bags and toss them in the water. I'm a purist, so I love to throw the entire herb, flower or vegetable in the bath. It makes me feel like Cleopatra in ancient Egypt or a wicked harlot getting ready for her Roman Soldier. However, if you do decide to use actual flowers or vegetables, make sure you have a strainer on your drain.

Below are a couple of "financial baths" that can help you get a quick money fix.

All Purpose Aura Cleaner: Put half a cup of sea salts or Epsom salts plus half a cup of baking soda in the bath to purify your aura and clear it of all negative attachments so that you are surrounded once again by a rainbow of opportunities.

Barley Water Bath: Barley water is used to dispel evil with a capital E. This is definitely the bath to take if you are feeling haunted by something unseemly or if something of a supernatural origin is acting as a prosperity block. Boil whole barley in a pot until it is soft. Drain the barley and save the water. Pour the water into the bath. Evil spirits will run like hell.

Chamomile: Chamomile not only relaxes you, but also draws money to you. Many preparations for a chamomile bath are available commercially but you can make an infusion out of the flower buds or even throw the buds directly into the bath. I do not advise this if you are allergic to ragweed.

Ginger-Lime Bath: You can buy this bath mixture commercially (Ombra), or you can cut up some ginger and lime and make an infusion in a pot. The ginger helps you relax and focus and the lime is for self-control and discipline. This is a great bath for those who need to "get down to business fast."

Honeysuckle: You can buy this as a bubble bath or just throw the flowers into the tub. Honeysuckle attracts

wealth, riches, honors, marriage proposals and treasures. This is one way to draw the bird to the blossom.

Lavender: Lavender corresponds to the planet Mercury
and is used to improve communication, attract happiness and achieve piece of mind. Many commercial
preparations are available, but throwing in a few fresh
buds might bring you a wealthy and generous lover.

Lucky Green Tea Bath: For this bath you will need an
Earl Grey tea bag. Earl Grey Tea contains the spice
bergamot, which draws luck and money. Or you can
buy bergamot essential oil, bubble bath or gel. In a
pinch, place the teabag over the bathtub faucet and
run a hot bath. Add a bit of food coloring to the water
to tint it green—the color of money. Then immerse
yourself in the water, saying positive things such as
"millions of dollars are coming to me as I speak."
Don't be greedy and stay in too long or add too much
food coloring lest you turn into a leprechaun.

Pineapple: Pineapple juice is used to attract luck, money
and wealth. If you are a purist, you can throw nine
chunks of raw fruit into your bath. However, I warn
you that it is pretty messy. Some people prefer to
throw in dry pineapple, add a spoonful of juice or
make an infusion from the rinds. Immersing yourself
for a couple of minutes should make you luckier
than a leprechaun.

Rosemary: Rosemary is a powerful "wish granting"
herb. Ombra makes an excellent commercial bath,
but you can make an infusion if you have dried rosemary in your spice jar or put a drop of essential oil in
your bath (use only one drop as rosemary is strong
and can irritate the skin). A rosemary bath uplifts the
spirits. It also creates lust, attracts love and improves
communication skills. Rosemary also corresponds to

the Virgin Mary, so if you are in need of a lucky break, a rosemary bath may bring you mercy.

Saffron Bath: Saffron is sacred to the Moon and the Fertility Goddess, Ashtoreth. It is an expensive spice but you need only a couple of strands in your bath water to turn it a yellow color. Don't add too much or you will turn yellow yourself. Either make an infusion first or add just one strand. Saffron is used to purify individuals before healing rituals, to increase psychic powers and to attract love, prosperity and strength.

Sage Bath: Sage is the herb of wisdom. Brew the herb and pour the liquid into your bath. Some companies (like Ombra and Kneipp) make a sage bath, but you can also buy it in tea bags. This is a good bath to take before studying for a test or if you are trying to find a solution to a problem.

Bathroom Magic

Believe it or not, the bathroom is one of the most magical rooms in your house. Your makeup box and medicine chest can be a treasure trove of tools. The bathtub and shower are a wonderful place to conduct cleansing and attraction rituals, and the toilet can be a handy mechanism for flushing away negativity.

Here are some examples of positive magic that can be performed in your powder room. First of all, make sure that your bathroom is clean and that the mirror doesn't face or reflect a drain or toilet. According to Feng Shui wisdom, this prevents your money from disappearing.

Need to do well in that job interview? Spearmint (a herb ruled by Mercury) will make you more eloquent, witty and charming. Toothpaste or mouthwash flavored with spearmint might help you find exactly the right words to say to impress your boss.

Green soap can also be used as a visualization aid to remove prosperity blocks. As the soap dissolves, picture it representing the hostility that stands between you and great riches. An advanced version of this spell would be to carve the soap with a personal symbol that represents the problem and run it under the tap on and off for a couple of days until the bar is completely dissolved.

You can also use various soaps and bath gels to achieve different magical results. Remember that the magic lies in your intention as you use the product. A honeysuckle bath can bring money to your hands. Orange soap promotes joy, fun and creative opportunities. Rosemary-scented soap or bath gel is used to improve business and communication. Lime-scented soap or bath gel is used to stop obsessive thoughts and help you concentrate on the task at hand.

Then there is the fine art of flushing your troubles away. Write your financial problem on a piece of toilet paper or tissue and, while keeping your thoughts on the problem, flush it down the toilet. If you want a more dramatic effect, throw a bit of baking soda mixed with vinegar so that the toilet temporarily represents a bubbling cauldron. Goodbye, troubles! Goodbye, sorrows!

Magical Wreaths

A wreath is like a ring. It represents the Universal Circle ("Let the circle be unbroken..." as the song goes) and also the circulation of love, wealth and prosperity for you and your neighbors. A wreath is usually hung on the front door, over the fireplace or laid on the dining-room table to commemorate special occasions or the changing of the seasons.

To make the frame for your wreath you will need

strong thread, glue and branches from the appropriate tree. Try to make your wreath from branches you find on the ground, however, if you can't, be sure to thank the tree whose branches your have cut. Alternatively, you can buy a pre-fabricated frame at a local craft store. Most craft stores sell circular frames made from varnished grapevines that look quite natural.

A wreath can be complicated and hung with a cornucopia of herbs, fruits and flowers or it can be as simple as a bunch of pussy willows braided together to form a circle. Below are a few suggestions for different wreaths you can make to attract prosperity.

Abundance Wreath: This little wreath is beautiful, classy and fragrant. Use a grapevine armature and intertwine it with sprigs of basil, rosemary, thyme, parsley or sage. All of these herbs draw wealth to the home. You can also attach small oranges or kumquats to the wreath. For an added dash of spice, pierce the oranges with fragrant cloves—an orange stuck with cloves is an ancient way to quickly draw money.

Chinese Prosperity Drawing Wreath: Use fresh or dried red, orange and yellow chrysanthemums, which symbolize autumn and money. To make this wreath you can use a Styrofoam board backing and affix the flowers with pins. Or you can tie them to a grapevine armature. Decorate the wreath with red ribbons.

Cornucopia of the Gods Wreath: Take pine or spruce branches and twist them into a circle using wire and pliers if necessary. Decorating this wreath is not unlike decorating a Christmas tree, but you will be attaching pomegranates, oranges, walnuts, kumquats, pine cones, acorns, bay leaves and chocolate-covered coins. I prefer to use fresh materials, but you can use plastic grapes, strawberries or oranges. Finish this masterpiece off with gold, yellow and green ribbons.

Martha Stewart's Oshun Happiness Wreath: I stole this idea from Martha Stewart, who probably didn't realize she had invented something that would honor the African Goddess of the Rivers, Love and Wealth, Oshun. It is Oshun who takes care of relationships, love, money, and all the things that make life sweet. To make this wreath you will need straight pins or a glue gun and bags of pink, orange and yellow gumdrops. Use the pins (or glue) to press the candies onto a pre-cut styrofoam backing. The effect is a sunburst of joy. Finish off the wreath with a big bow made of pink, yellow and orange ribbons. Save this wreath to put on your mantelpiece. Oshun is not the only being that loves sugar. You don't want an army of birds and squirrels attacking your front door!

The Abundant Techno Witch

My favorite episode of *Bugs Bunny* is the one where Bugs turns into a witch and says: "We ride vacuum cleaners now."

It is true that technology can be used to cast a spell. For instance, one way to get rid of negative energy in your home is to sprinkle sage leaves or salt over the floor, and instead of sweeping, vacuum up all the bad vibrations. This is good practice when a nasty person has paid you a visit or a tragic event has taken place in your environment. The old way to cast a spell would be to sprinkle salt all over the floor and sweep the astral detritus away with a broom. Lightly sprinkling salt onto the floor and vacuuming your house in a counter-clockwise direction during a waning moon is a good practice. Another modern convenience, the common household drain, can be used to perform a "banishing spell." Every time you rinse out your sink, picture all the bad energy in your life going down the drain. Picture your burdens and bad habits swirling away. An automatic disposal unit can be used in a similar way. Potatoes, which have been used throughout history to make poppets (crude forms of voodoo dolls), can be carved into the shape of a person or into a symbol of the thing you want removed from your life and crushed in the garbage disposal. But you don't have to spend time carving symbols out of potatoes and wasting perfectly good food. Whenever you mulch, crush, destroy or rinse something, or throw it down the drain, visualize a problem in your life disappearing along with the waste.

The toaster is also a Techno Witch's best friend. With a knife, lightly carve a symbol representing what you wish—such as the amount of money you need—into a slice of bread or a frozen waffle. The toasting of the bread represents the cosmos "warming up to the idea." When the toast or waffle is ready, spread it first with butter to smooth your way, then with honey to make sure your wishes "stick" to you. Marmalade is also good for attracting money into the home.

In the old days, witches used a mortar and pestle to grind magical elements in order to release their essence. Today, you can use a blender, chopper or even a coffee grinder to achieve the same results. All cooking practices are a form of magic. The blender is a useful Techno Witch tool for gathering and banishing energy and creating love potions. You can bring money into your home by pulverizing spinach with cream to make prosperity soup.

The stove has always been a witch's best friend but

the microwave is the ultimate tool for the Techno Witch. The microwave is great for producing accelerated results. One prosperity ritual is to cook a bag of microwave popcorn and while each kernel pops, yell out a wish. You can do this on the stove as well, but the microwave brings faster results.

You've heard of applied science—well, how about applied Magic? The personal computer is just a tool, so in theory you should be able to apply ancient traditions to modern ways. Here are a few ways that you can use your PC to practice metaphysics.

The Gods, Goddesses and energies that oversee the running of your computer include Mercury (Hermes), the God of Communication, Ariadne (the Weaver), the Archangel Jophiel (the Angel of Illumination), Vachu (the Hindu goddess of Mystic Speech) and Chango, the African God of Thunderbolts. If you are experiencing computer problems, burning a candle or some incense can help. Light a red and blue candle to honor Mercury (for server and e-mail problems), a purple candle to honor Ariadne (for site problems), some Temple or Lotus incense to access Vachu (who can help with forwarding files), a yellow candle to access the wisdom of the Archangel Jophiel (to figure out how to get a program running) or a red candle to honor Chango (for problems with electricity).

When sending a resumé or an important file, practice a bit of magic by creating a symbol to hide somewhere in the file or e-mail. This symbol should represent success or prosperity. For instance, "$" would be an obvious one. Try being creative by using a series of letters, numbers or symbols that are significant to you. Or create a sigil to attach to your e-mails. Creating a sigil is easy. Take a phrase such as "Money, Come To Me" and shorten it to "MCTM" or "mctm" and put it in your tag before you send an important document. There are many sites on the Internet that teach you how to make a more obscure sigil using numbers and letters—just type the word **sigil** into your search engine. Once you create the sigil, enlarge it to twenty-four-point and "charge it" by focusing your intent onto the symbol. Keep the master sigil in a file and attach a nine-point version to the bottom of files or e-mails.

You can use naming and retrieving of files to bring more luck, prosperity and love into your life. To do this you need to create a folder and fill it with files that contain one word such as LOVE, MONEY or LUCK. Inside each of these files, include a list of words that relate to your goal. For instance, in the file marked MONEY write things such as Quick Cash, Relief From Debt, Prosperity, New Car or whatever you desire. Put these files on your desktop, so that each time you start up your computer you retrieve the magical energy of the words inside the files.

Turn your mouse into a Magic Mouse by storing it overnight inside a "sleeping bag" that contains a coin, a sprig of rosemary and a paper heart. An old saying goes "a mouse in the house brings luck to the house." Every time you click your mouse, the energies represented by what is stored in its "sleeping bag" will infuse your life with lucky energy.

Another good way to manifest magic is to use your screensaver. Try to choose imagery that supports your magical intent. For instance, images of waterfalls and running water symbolize money, images of flowers represent love, and images of clouds or the sun represent the acquisition of experience and wisdom.

Never underestimate the power of a password. When you choose login names or passwords, try to choose names that attract positive energy. For instance, the password name "fatdope" might just attract more fat dopes into your sphere. Remember the cosmic principle of "like attracts like."

Practice your computer magic at noon or on Sundays.

Smudging

Some practitioners believe that a ritual will not work until a place has been cleansed of negative energies or blessed through the use of smoke.

An Aboriginal Canadian friend who teaches at the Whispering Song Teaching Lodge in Toronto explained that physical or emotional healing cannot take place until the person is cleansed of any of the following conditions:

1) Emotions such as resentment, bitterness, envy, jealousy or guilt.
2) Negative thoughts about others or about the past or future.
3) Emotions such as grief, hatred or desire.
4) Evil spirits.
5) Attachments or negative energy sent by other people.

In most Aboriginal traditions, a sweat lodge (basically a tent, teepee or cave filled with heat and smoke) is used to cure the sick person of the above conditions. In ancient Rome, buildings called purgatoriums were used for the same purpose; these were sacred spaces in which the god or spirits could lift negative entities and energies from an individual without interference from others. Many indigenous cultures throughout the world burn herbs, plants and resins to accomplish the same purpose.

In some cultures the smoke is taken in the hands and rubbed over the body to blacken it. This is where the modern-day practice got its nickname; smudging.

Below is a list of common herbs, plants, grasses and resins that are commonly used in smudging ceremonies. Light these substances and carry a bundle around the home in a counter-clockwise circle to cleanse it. I recommend cleansing the body outside, since sage can burn quickly and create a lot of whirling smoke that can easily set off the fire alarm.

Sage Sprigs: The most common substance used for cleansing is sage. The word "sage" comes from the Latin word "salvia," which means "to heal." Varieties of sage such as white sage and mugwort are used for cleansing and protection. Combining branches of pine and white sage and burning them attracts prosperity.

Cedar and Juniper branches: These evergreen boughs have been used throughout history to help cleanse, purify and protect people's belongings. Sometimes brooms are made from these branches to "sweep" a home during a house blessing.

Sweetgrass: This musty-smelling grass is used to drive out bad influences and draw good ones into the home. It is often used after a prayer or ritual to "hold the magic" in its place.

Copal: This aromatic plant resin is used mainly in South American rituals. A touch of the strongly scented smoke from burning copal is thought to cleanse and purify any object or person.

Frankincense and Myrrh: These "Biblical" resins are used for ceremonies in Europe, Africa and the Middle East. When the resins are burned together they balance the masculine and feminine energies in a dwelling. Either material will draw blessings into a home.

Tobacco: Tobacco is burned to send prayers upwards to the Creator who will hear and answer them. Burning tobacco along with sage, cedar or sweetgrass enhances the magical intentions of the smudge.

Smudges and resins can be bought commercially from occult, New Age or regular gift shops. You can also use a feather or a branch to waft the smoke in the desired direction.

Smudging creates negative ions in the air that remove static and render a positive atmosphere. After a smudging ceremony people usually feel good, and a space for the free flowing of positive energies and prayers is manifested.

Simple Money-Drawing Rituals

Although I am not a big believer in magic monkeys, these spells have been known to draw prosperity into people's lives. The danger with spell-working is that we often put too much faith in an object rather than in a Higher Power or in ourselves. However, my experience as a spiritual counselor is that it can sometimes take years for an individual to reach a place where he or she doesn't need magical tools to realize a dream.

The following rituals are the classic ones used for money-drawing, wealth and prosperity. Unlike candle burning, some rituals involve a little more concentration and appreciation for the theatrical.

Quick Money-Drawing Ritual: Scratch the amount of
money you need and your full name into the side of

a green candle. Anoint it with cinnamon oil (for speed). Let the candle burn all the way down.

Trinka Five: The Trinka Five chant is believed to be Romanian or Gypsy in origin.

According to legend, the words Trinka Five hold such powerful money-drawing qualities that it is enough to repeat the phrase three times in your head in order to manifest money. It is also thought that rubbing your hands together rapidly, while repeating "Trinka Five" expedites the cash.

A more complicated use of Trinka Five is illustrated by the following permutation:

Place a bowl or a cup in a prominent area in your home. Hold three coins in your dominant hand and recite,

"Trinka five, Trinka five,
Generous spirits come alive,
Money grow and money thrive,
Fairies of the Trinka five."

Deposit the coins in the container. Repeat this ritual for nine consecutive days. After the ninth day, perform the ritual once a week until you are financially solvent.

The Penny Dance: This is a simple ritual of Chinese origin. Choose a goblet, vase or pretty vessel of some kind. Every day add a penny to this vessel to ensure the proper circulation of money in your life. When the vessel is full, remove the pennies and begin the ritual again.

The Goblet Spell: Select a favorite goblet or wine glass. On the night of the full moon fill half your goblet with mineral or spring water and drop in a silver coin. Position the goblet so that the light of the full moon shines onto the silver coin. As you perform this ritual, repeat:

"Goddess Moon hear my request,
Do for me your financial best,
Fill this cup with plenty and love,
As below, so above."

Bury the coin near the front door of your house and pour the water to on a favorite plant.

The Red Envelope Ritual: This is a Chinese tradition that relates to the concept of tithing. Every time you receive a windfall, take nine pennies, $9 or $90 and put the money in a red envelope. You can find Chinese envelopes, often decorated with images of pears, money ingots and goldfish in Chinese stores, or you can buy regular red envelopes. Place the appropriate amount of money in the red envelopes and leave them on the street for other individuals to find. It helps to write "God Bless You," or "Free Lucky Money, May It Multiply For You" on the outside of the envelope. You may also make out nine checks to favorite charities, stuff them inside red envelopes and mail them out. This ritual represents the free circulation of money in your life.

For Self-Confidence and Success: This is a good spell to perform before an important job interview.

Light a blue candle in front of a mirror. Sit at the mirror, stare into your own eyes and count to twenty-one.

Ask the Powers That Be to place a circle of gold light around you. Repeat your Christian name or names twenty-one times.

Then speak your wish and repeat it twenty-one times.

Blow out the candle and await success.

Prosperity Pomander: Take one large orange, lemon,

lime or kumquat. Citrus fruits represent joy and abundance. Take approximately eighteen inches of green ribbon and wrap it several times around the fruit. When it is wrapped, tie the ribbon in a knot leaving enough extra to hang the fruit from a hook. Use stick pins to insert as many cloves into it as possible. Hang the pomander near the front door to draw prosperity while chanting "Fruit and cloves, my money now grows."

Dream-Working Ritual: On the eve of the New Moon, write your wish on a clean piece of paper. Light a white candle and turn off all the lights. Think about the fulfillment of your wish for several minutes, then say:

"As I sleep tonight, may the Divine Imagination grant my wish. I ask for (amount of money in dollars). I thank you in advance for the blessings that are mine by Divine Right. Amen."

Burn the piece of paper with the wish on it in the flame of the candle.

Repeat this ritual at the same time for fourteen consecutive nights—until the moon is full.

Good Luck Spell: This spell is traditionally used for windfalls and luck in gambling.

Hold a tiger's eye stone in your right hand and a favorite silver charm in the left. Make sure you like this charm as you will be carrying it around for a few days. Good choices are ankhs, crucifixes, pentagrams and acorns. Meditate for a few moments on the amount of money you need to fill your demand.

Sprinkle nutmeg and allspice on the charm. Then say:

"Prosperity Charm bring me good luck."

Keep the charm with you at all times. When you feel it necessary, recharge the charm again with this spell.

To Increase Business: Crumble three bay leaves into a square of aluminum foil. Add cinnamon powder and seven pennies. Roll the foil into a ball and place it inside your cash register.

Monopoly Money Ritual: Anoint a green taper candle with mint, cinnamon or honeysuckle oil. Three days before the Full Moon, carve several dollar signs into the side of the candle. Take monopoly money and count out the amount of dollars that you would like to receive. Light the candle. Shuffle the money and place it in front of the candle. Think about this money for nine minutes and snuff out the candle.

Repeat this procedure the next two nights, until the night of the Full Moon. On this night, let the candles burn down completely.

Financial Request Spell: Place a red candle inside the U of an iron horseshoe. Write the amount of money that you need on a piece of paper with green ink. Fold the paper four times and as you burn it in the flame, make your financial request.

Spell to Keep Your Job: To ensure that you do not lose your job, buy nine pecans. Pecans are used frequently in money and prosperity spells. Shell each pecan and eat it slowly while visualizing yourself working and enjoying your job. Take the shells, wrap them in a green piece of cloth or a green plastic bag and hide it somewhere in your workplace where the shells can't be found or removed.

The Lucky Five Money Bottle: In a tall bottle combine: five pennies, five dimes, five quarters, five kernels of dried corn, five teaspoons of wheat flour, five sesame seeds, five cinnamon sticks, five cloves, five allspice cloves and five whole pecans.

Cap the bottle tightly, shake it and say:

"Copper and herbs,
Silver and grain,
Bring to me
Financial Gain."

Place the bottle in the southwest corner of your kitchen.

Knot Money Spell: If you have short hair or no hair, substitute green thread or yarn for this spell.

Take nine long strands of hair from your hair brush. Rub the hair between your palms to form a cord. Tie nine knots in this cord in the following order. The numbers represent where the knots should be tied:

—1—6—4—8—3—7—5—9—2—

Tie the first knot at the left end of the hair cord, the second knot at the right end of the hair cord, the third knot in the middle and so on.

As you tie the knots, visualize your financial needs being met. When you are done, throw the hair cord to the wind, and thank the spirits for all the blessings you will receive in the future.

Tarot Spell to Attract Clients: On the night of the Full Moon, take the ace, ten, nine and seven of diamonds out of a brand new deck of regular playing cards. Anoint each card with orange, patchouli or cinnamon oil (or commercial money-drawing oil,) bind them together with a green ribbon and place them in your purse, pocket or cash register or under your phone and computer. Re-anoint the cards every Full Moon to recharge the spell.

Prosperity Pot-Pourri: You will need two cinnamon sticks, two teaspoons of sliced or ground ginger, five teaspoons of whole cardamom seeds, and one tablespoon of ground nutmeg.

Stir this mixture clockwise nine times with your finger while envisioning financial success. Place the mixture in a jar with no lid and hide it in your kitchen cupboard.

Path to Success Spell: This spell can help you achieve a goal quickly. Place a green candle in the southwest corner of your home and a purple candle in the northwest corner. Light the purple candle. Visualize how you will achieve your goal. After nine minutes, take the purple candle and quickly walk straight to the green candle on the other side of the house. Light the green candle and let it burn for nine minutes. Imagine how you will feel after you achieve your goal. Snuff the candles out gently and bury the ends in your backyard.

To Remove Prosperity Blocks: The surgeon general is not going to agree with this, but a cup of coffee and a cigarette can help to eliminate bad energies from your home.

For an intense effect, burn a little ground coffee mixed with tobacco on a small piece of charcoal in an incense burner. You can buy coin-shaped pieces of charcoal in any occult store. They spark a bit when you light them but they are perfect for burning herbs and other substances inside brass incense burners. The ground coffee helps to remove heavy thoughts (created by you or anyone else) from the environment. The tobacco protects you physically and frees you from negative influences that might be sent to you either consciously or unconsciously by others.

Balloon Money Ritual: I love balloon spells. They are so liberating! Blow up a balloon in a color that is sympathetic with your desire. Use a green, gold or blue balloon for money; a one pink for joy and fertility; or an orange one for happiness and fulfillment. There are two versions of this spell. You can blow up the balloon yourself, make a mark on it that represents your desire (such as a chalice or money sign,) and keep it floating in the air as long as possible. Each time you tap the balloon you build energy towards the manifestation of your wish. Or you can buy a helium-filled balloon (don't use a pen to mark the balloon or it will pop in your face) and release it into the sky.

Samantha's Master Bay Leaf Ritual: I would like to share a spell derived from an ancient Greek ritual for prosperity and fertility. As you may recall, ancient Mediterranean kings and queens used to wear garlands of bay leaves as crowns. Bay leaves, and often bayberry leaves, are also used in Alexandrian magic to draw success in business and finances. I like this ritual because it involves writing down your wishes. The writing down of your wishes on 108 bay leaves works in the same way as a positive affirmation. Stating your goals and desires allows you to properly manifest them in real life. Every year I pull out my old bay leaves and sort through them and I am always astounded by how many of my wishes have been granted.

To perform this ritual you will need: a package of whole bay leaves; a blank check; a pen with gold, silver or green ink; cinnamon incense; a green, orange, yellow or gold candle (whichever color attracts you the most); orange oil, bergamot, or Horn of Plenty oil; an envelope and a pretty ribbon.

This ritual is meant for multiple wishes and it is best to do it when you have at least two hours to spare in meditation. It is most effective when performed ten days before or after New Year's day, or on the day itself. It is also a wonderful ritual to perform during the solstices or on your birthday.

First of all, take a bath in your favorite bubbles (Claxon, take me away!) and enter a calm and peaceful state. If you like, play some steady rhythmic music—anything that puts you into a bit of a trance.

Begin by lighting the cinnamon incense. Cinnamon is related to the planet Mercury and symbolizes communication and quick results. Next, scratch your name and birth date on the side of the candle. Put the candle on a plate wrapped in tin foil to represent the moon. Then take the blank check and write the amount of money that you would like to earn this year or the amount you need to get out of trouble using the colored pen. Make the check payable to yourself.

The idea is to make the check as pretty as possible. Decorate it with lucky symbols such as dollar signs, hearts or flowers so that the money will be brought to you with a sense of joy. Once you are happy with your check and have signed and endorsed it, anoint all four corners with one or more of the oils listed above. To make the check even more personal, add a dab of your favorite perfume.

Place the check under the foil-wrapped dish. Light the candle and say:

"In the name of the I Am That I Am I pray to the Archangels and their legions of light, I pray to the blessed Virgin and her angels of compassion for the following assistance and blessings."

Now open the package of bay leaves. This spell can be done in two ways—in a really dramatic way or in a more efficient manner, depending on how much time you have. When I did this on my birthday I used 108 bay leaves (or fragments of leaves since they sometimes crumble in the package) because 108 is a magic number, but you can use fewer if you like.

As the candle and the incense burn, write on each bay leaf a single word that represents each thing you would like to happen. For instance, if you are looking for immigration status, write the word "citizenship" on the bay leaf. If you owe the dentist money, write "dentist bill paid." If you would like a lover to return, write "lover returns." Each leaf will have a wish written on it: "high paying job," "security" or "soulmate." Place the leaves in a circle around the candle and wish until you are exhausted. Since this spell usually takes a while, most people find that before they know it the candle has burned down.

After you have written a wish, it helps if you "let it go" and resign yourself to the fact that the Higher Powers will take care of it.

After you have written all your wishes, say: "I consider this done in this hour, in full power according to the will of God, helping all and harming none. Amen."

When the candle burns out, take the leaves and the check and put them in an envelope. Seal the envelope, tie it with ribbon, kiss it and put it in a safe place. Don't look at this again for a year. Just be assured that everything in the Universe is unfolding as it should.

Chapter Eleven

Kitchen Witchery

If you are what you think, you certainly are what you eat. Cooking is the most ancient form of magic there is. Here are some recipes I have collected over the years that will bring prosperity.

Greenback Salad

Shred lettuce into dollar bill-sized pieces. Drizzle them with olive oil (to attract money) and sprinkle with salt (for grounding and purification). Concentrate on your money goals while you consume the greens.

May Day Pancakes

Beltane (also known as May Day) is a magical Celtic holiday that celebrates love, fertility and new beginnings. Try making these delicious May Day Maple Pancakes. But, you don't have to wait until May to enjoy the prosperous attributes of this delicious breakfast dish.

You'll need:

Instant pancake mix

A quarter cup of coarsely ground hazelnuts (pecans or almonds will do)

Pure maple syrup

The rind of one orange

A quart of strawberries

Two tablespoons of sugar

Two scoops of vanilla ice cream

Slice the strawberries lengthwise so that each slice resembles a heart. Strawberries represent fidelity, love, sex and joy. Sprinkle the sugar over the strawberry hearts and leave them to soak in a bowl. The sugar will naturally draw the juices out of the strawberries and make a watery pink sauce.

Follow the directions on the pancake mix to make pancake batter. Add the nuts. The hazelnuts reinforce the idea of productivity and fertility in the near future. As you add the nuts to the batter, think about cold hard lumps of cash coming to you. Grate the orange rind into the batter and think about how blessings will be showered on you this summer, like sprinkles of joy from heaven.

If you can, shape the pancakes into hearts or coins.

When the pancakes are cooked, spoon some vanilla ice cream on top (the vanilla and cream represents smooth sailing over the next couple of months). Top this with strawberries and some of the pink sauce. Then drizzle maple syrup over the whole thing and enjoy. Maple syrup commemorates the movement of sap through the trees in spring and the life it brings to all the boughs. The idea is to consume this delicious concoction while thinking about how you may branch out in your life.

Enchanted Omelets

Prepare this dish as you would an ordinary omelet— except this is no ordinary omelet, it is a ritual!

Chop and sauté spinach, mushrooms and onions; these are all sacred foods of Ishtar, the Babylonian Earth Goddess. Take eight eggs (eight is the number of prosperity). Crack each egg into a mixing bowl while thinking about eight different things you would like to accomplish by next month. Think of each shiny yolk as a prospect for the future. Add salt and pepper for purification, and parsley flakes for good luck. Now beat these eggs in a counterclockwise direction until they are foamy (about eighty-eight times).

Pour the eggs into a pan and add the vegetables. Before you flip the omelet add any kind of cheese. Cheese represents joy, health and things coming to fruition. Orange cheeses, like cheddar, will add an extra dose of joy, but feta or mozzarella will do.

Serve with potatoes (for earthy energies) and toast.

Sunshine Carrots

This vivid dish is said to arouse the fiery energies associated with the Sun Gods. The bright orange of the carrots invokes love, joy, health and energy and helps to see things in a more optimistic light.

Take five cups of diced carrots and boil until tender. Place in a blender or food processor and blend until smooth. Add 1/4 cup cream, 1/4 cup butter, 1/4 teaspoon powder and puree until smooth. The magic in this dish relies mainly in its presentation.

Pour the puree into the center of a serving platter. Place a dollop of sour cream in the center. Take two cups of baby carrots and arrange them in rays around the carrot sun to form the shape of a solar disk. While you do this, think about what a "hot" item you are whether it comes to love, social life or business.

Prosperity Pesto Sauce

In India, basil is considered a herb that brings happiness. In Italy and Greece, the herb is believed to bring wealth. Pine nuts are considered "nuggets of wisdom." Olive oil represents the flow of money and cheese binds your treasures to you.

In a blender place:
2 cups fresh basil leaves
3/4 cup grated Parmesan cheese
3/4 cup olive oil

5 cloves garlic
2 tablespoons pine nuts

Pulverize the mixture in a blender until smooth. Serve over any kind of cooked pasta. Before eating give thanks for all the riches and blessings that you already enjoy.

Lucky Coffee

This recipe is for gamblers. Before you go off to the casino or the racetrack, brew a cup of coffee. Put the filter and ground coffee in the basket as usual and then add a smidgen of cinnamon, (the Kitchen Witch's equivalent of money-attracting powder) and a couple of grains of nutmeg. Nutmeg has been used for centuries to increase prophetic powers. Drinking this coffee will not only keep your powers of concentration sharp, it will also aid your intuition in making the right choices.

Jupiter Platter

This is a dish I recommend you enjoy on November 13th, the day of the Roman Festival called the Feast of Jupiter. It is the ancient equivalent of Thanksgiving. Jupiter is the god of plenty, bounty and generosity. To re-enact Thanksgiving as Romans did in Rome, prepare a feast consisting of the following:

Barbecued chicken
Rye Bread
Olives
Honey
Dates
Pomegranates
Goat's Milk

Include jugs and jugs of RED WINE! Make sure you eat with your fingers, laugh a lot, slurp and burp in appreciation of the harvest that takes place every year.

Confetti or Buddha Rice

Many versions of this dish exist but it is thought to have originated in China. The cherries are for good fortune; the lily is a symbol of luck; the chrysanthemums are for wealth; the lychees represent fertility; the dates represent longevity; the oranges stand for joy; and the plums for good health. Since this dish resembles confetti, it is a wonderful dish to welcome in the New Year. It was invented to honor the Buddha and thought to enhance visions, dreams and the power of prophecy. You will need:

3 cups cooked rice
1 cup chopped lychee fruit
1/2 cup pitted cherries
1/2 cup pitted dates
1/2 cup diced plums
2 oranges peeled and separated into segments
1/2 cup sugar
1 teaspoon dried lotus, violet or chrysanthemum flowers
1/4 teaspoon cinnamon
1 teaspoon ground ginger
1 tablespoon soft butter

Preheat oven to 225 degrees Fahrenheit. Combine all the ingredients except the rice and butter with one cup of water in a saucepan. Simmer until a syrup forms. Spread half of the rice in the bottom of a greased pan and dot this with half of the butter. Cover this with half the fruit mixture (like making a lasagna). Cover with the rest of the rice and repeat with the remaining butter and fruit. Bake about ten minutes until thoroughly heated.

Peachy Keen Potion

In China, peaches represent fertility, health, longevity and well-being. The vanilla is to sweeten and smooth your path in the future and the honey is for strength, discipline and stamina. Cloverleaf honey is thought to draw money. Orange blossom honey is thought to draw romance.

8 ounces of yogurt
6 or 7 frozen peach segments
Honey (clover or orange blossom is good)
Vanilla
1/3 cup spring water

Place all the ingredients in a blender and push the "Destroy" button. As you watch the ingredients pulverize, think about all the good things that a positive attitude can create in your life.

Mulled Wine

This is an ancient traditional holiday drink that originates in England and Iceland. Its name translates as "a salute to prosperity and good luck." This recipe makes sixteen servings.

6 cups dry red wine or apple wine
10 cups apple cider
1/2 cup packed brown sugar
2 teaspoons whole cloves
2 teaspoons whole allspice
2 large cinnamon sticks
2 oranges

Combine the wine, cider, sugar, cloves, allspice and cinnamon in a large pot. Heat over a medium flame until it comes to a low boil. Cover and reduce heat to low. Simmer this mixture for twenty minutes, strain, and pour into a large punch bowl. Garnish with orange slices or cherries.

Ojo Drink

This drink from the Far East was enjoyed in Biblical days. It was believed to connect the physical self to the Higher Self and raise vibrations to connect with the right path in life. It was thought to brighten the eyes so that one could see all things with clarity. The almond, honey and dates possess money-drawing qualities.

Combine half of a cup of goat's or cow's milk, half of a cup of almond milk, one tablespoon of honey and three or four chopped dates. Add a few icecubes. Blend until smooth.

Chapter Twelve

Feng Shui for Prosperity

Feng Shui is the ancient art of furniture placement to achieve the best of luck. The first law of prosperity is to thoroughly clean your home and clear it of all clutter in order to clear the air, prevent prosperity blocks and allow positive chi (life force) to circulate freely.

The Chinese place a large bowl or aquarium filled with sixteen goldfish—eight gold and eight black ones—near the front door of their homes and businesses. The fish are believed to bring money and good fortune. If one of these fish dies, it means that the misfortune that was supposed to strike you felled the fish instead.

An orange or lemon tree placed by the front door or in the southwest corner of your home or office is thought to increase business and general prosperity. The more green fruit the tree bears, the better your business will be.

Protecting your home from the arrows of outrageous misfortune is as easy as placing a small mirror, preferably eight-sided, in the front window of your home facing the street. The Chinese call these mirrors Pa Kua and you can find them in the local Chinatown section of your city. However, in my experience, any mirror will do. It is important to keep the entrance to your home brightly lit, freshly painted and clean of litter, so that you do not attract intruders, predators, vacuum cleaner salesmen or any bad energy to your front door. For additional protection, you can also nail an iron horseshoe, right side up, inside the front door. The U shape represents your luck and embraces it so it doesn't flow away from you.

Want to be famous? Artists, writers and actors will appreciate this hint. Make sure the southwestern corner of your home is brightly lit and decorated with triangular, cone-shaped or pyramid-shaped items. The southwest corner is a good place to hang diplomas, prizes and acknowledgements. Objects made from feathers, leather, wood and bone are also helpful in this area.

In China, the stove is considered a symbol of prosperity, and the more burners you have on your stove, the more fortunate you are considered to be. To "double" the number of burners on your stove, place an angled mirror above it to reflect eight burners instead of the usual four or place ten long thin mirrors beneath the dials and buttons to achieve the same effect.

One way to lose prosperous energy is to leave you cupboard doors or dresser drawers wide open. Make a habit of shutting them tight right after you remove an object. Always keep the lid of your toilet shut and your closet doors closed. Toilets, closets and cupboards are thought to trap "chi" or good energy that circulates prosperity and abundance in your life. Some diehard Feng Shui enthusiasts close the toilet lid before they flush, to avoid flushing their "wealth" down the drain.

Hang a small broom inside your front door to ensure all evil is "swept" away. This Feng Shui hint has its roots in gypsy magic.

In general, if you want to enhance your prosperity, make sure the southern, southeastern and northern sections of your home are kept clean and brightly lit. The south represents fame, the southeastern represents finances and the north stands for career matters. These areas can also be enhanced by the addition of mirrors, plants, chimes, fountains, rotating objects such as lava lamps, lucky statues, gemstones, awards, trophies, peacock feathers and flowers.

Chapter Thirteen

The Ten Cosmic Laws of Prosperity

We live in an abundant universe where there is a supply for every demand.

The heart must be aligned with the will and the soul in order to create good conditions for prosperity.

Think positive thoughts and you will manifest positive things.

Nothing prospers in a mind or home that is cluttered with doubt or fear.

Money is not a possession; it is an energy that is meant to be circulated throughout the economy to create prosperity.

The loaner must forgive all debts after seven years.

Ten percent of everything you own should be tithed to a charity.

Prosperity is the ability to realize that you do not want what is not yours by Divine Right.

If you lose something, have faith that it will be replaced by its equivalent or better. It is always darkest before the dawn.

What God has done for others He can do for you.